3/97

PERSPECTIVES

A Multicultural Portrait of

The Vietnam War

By David K. Wright

BENCHMARK BOOKS

MARSHALL CAVENDISH
NEW YORK

Cover: A small segment of the Vietnam Veterans Memorial in Washington, D.C., a wall that dramatically honors Americans who were killed or listed as missing during the Vietnam War. There are 58,196 names inscribed on the wall, although the exact number of dead and missing may never be known.

Benchmark Books
Marshall Cavendish Corporation
99 White Plains Road
Tarrytown, New York 10591-9001, U.S.A.

© Marshall Cavendish Corporation, 1996

Edited, designed, and produced by Water Buffalo Books, Milwaukee

Editorial consultant: Richard Taylor, History Department (Adjunct), the University of Wisconsin-Parkside

Picture Credits: © The Bettmann Archive: 52; © Reuters/Bettmann: 9 (top), 13, 73, 75; Courtesy of Mark J. Sachner: 57 (bottom); © UPI/Bettmann: Cover, 6, 8, 9 (bottom), 10, 11 (both), 12 (both), 14, 16, 18, 20, 21, 22, 24, 25, 26, 28, 29, 30, 32, 33, 34, 35, 36, 38, 39, 40 (both), 41, 42, 43, 44, 45, 47, 48, 49, 50, 53, 54, 55, 56 (both), 57 (top), 58, 59, 60, 61, 62, 63, 64, 66, 67, 68, 69, 70, 71, 72, 74

Library of Congress Cataloging-in-Publication Data

Wright. David K.
    A multicultural portrait of the Vietnam War / by David K. Wright.
        p.   cm. -- (Perspectives)
    Includes bibliographical references and index.
    ISBN 0-7614-0052-4 (lib. bdg.)
    1. Vietnamese Conflict, 1961-1975--United States--Juvenile literature. 2. Vietnam--History--1945-1975--
Juvenile literature. I. Title. III. Series: Perspectives (Benchmark Books (Firm))
    DS558.W74   1995
    959.704'3373--dc20   95-18817
                                                             CIP
                                                             AC

To PS – MS

Printed in Malaysia
Bound in the U.S.A.

CONTENTS

About *Perspectives*

Perspectives is a series of multicultural portraits of events and topics in U.S. history. Each volume examines these events and topics not only from the perspective of the white European-Americans who make up the majority of the U.S. population, but also from that of the nation's many people of color and other ethnic minorities, such as African-Americans, Asian-Americans, Hispanic-Americans, and American Indians. These people, along with women, have been given little attention in traditional accounts of U.S. history. And yet their impact on historical events has been great.

The terms *American Indian, Native American, Hispanic-American, Latino, Anglo-American, Black, African-American,* and *Asian-American,* like *European-American* and *white,* are used by the authors in this series to identify people of various national origins. Labeling people is a serious business, and what we call a group depends on many things. For example, a few decades ago it was considered acceptable to use the words *colored* or *Negro* to label people of African origin. Today, these words are outdated and often a sign of ignorance or outright prejudice. Some even consider *Black* less acceptable than *African-American* because it focuses on a person's skin color rather than national origins. And yet *Black* has many practical uses, especially to describe people whose origins are not only African but Caribbean or Latin American as well.

If we must label people, it is better to be as specific as possible. That is a goal of *Perspectives* — to be as precise and fair as possible in the labeling of people by race, ethnicity, national origin, or other factors, such as gender, sexual orientation, or disability. When necessary and possible, Americans of Mexican origin will be called *Mexican-Americans.* Americans of Irish origin will be called *Irish-Americans,* and so on. The same goes for American Indians: When possible, specific Indians are identified by their tribal names, such as Winnebago or *Mohawk.* But in a discussion of various Indian groups, tribal origins may not always be entirely clear, and so it may be more practical to use *American Indian,* a term that has widespread use among Indians and non-Indians alike.

Even within a group, individuals may disagree over the labels they prefer for their group: *Black* or *African-American? Hispanic* or *Latino? American Indian* or *Native American? White, Anglo,* or *European-American?* Different situations often call for different labels. The labels used in *Perspectives* represent an attempt to be fair, accurate, and perhaps most importantly, to be mindful of what people choose to call *themselves.*

A Note About *The Vietnam War*

Much can be learned from the war in Vietnam, particularly from a multicultural point of view:

• First, minority soldiers may have had different concerns than the white majority. For example, Native Americans volunteered for the U.S. Marines in large numbers during the Vietnam War in part because of their warrior tradition. The unpopularity of the war left surviving Indian veterans puzzled. Was their patriotism taken for granted? Had love of flag and love of country gone out of style? Here were American Indians taking responsibility in something that was suddenly wrong.

African-Americans had other concerns. Because there was so much unrest back in the United States, soldiers in Vietnam frequently worried about the well-being of their families. A lanky enlisted man in the U.S. Army's Ninth Infantry Division scanned *Stars and Stripes*, the official daily military newspaper, in 1967. He read with anxiety that his boyhood neighborhood in Detroit was the scene of summer rioting. If *Stars and Stripes* glossed over how bad things really were, shouldn't he be at home, defending his parents? This was only one small instance of troops mistrusting their government.

Other minorities had other misgivings, but they shared one postwar problem: They were treated as equals more in the military than they were back on U.S. streets. In fact, job discrimination contributed to the troubles some minorities had in readjusting to civilian society.

• Second, those who served, particularly in combat areas, realized that racial or ethnic differences disappeared in the heat of battle. Repeatedly, wire-service photos and newsreel film showed a mix of people fighting the enemy and struggling to save each other. Racial differences surfaced away from the battles, where soldiers had time on their hands. But under fire, no one analyzed race, ethnicity, or religion. Doctors, nurses, and aides worked as frantically to save a Mexican-American as they did to save a person whose European ancestors may have lived in New England for three hundred years.

• Third, it is hard to win a war if civilian society is against it. The conflict in Vietnam grew very slowly over many years, and opposition grew alongside it. Though most Americans believed communism to be a threat to democracy, they also came to believe that what was being fought in Vietnam was a civil war in which the United States had no stake.

• Fourth, no matter how negatively a war is viewed, there will be some citizens who believe that the country was right all along. In the case of the Vietnam War, many of the believers were in government. They so feared communism that they believed it had to be stopped wherever it appeared. These same Americans thought that the military was being held back, even though for several years increasing numbers of weapons and men were thrown into battle. Though they might not admit it, they also felt that winning the war was worth the lives of more than fifty-eight thousand of their fellow citizens.

An Army of the Republic of Vietnam (ARVN) soldier wears a helmet with a U.S. flag shortly before U.S. forces depart Vietnam in 1973. The entire burden of the war effort would shift to South Vietnam once the policy of "Vietnamization" took hold.

CHAPTER ONE

A Long and Complex War

Brenda Ford will never forget that cold day in February 1966. A police officer stopped at her house to tell the family that her brother Raymond had been killed in Vietnam. Brenda, just thirteen, had been spending time with friends a few blocks away. "I remember coming into the house," she said. "Everyone was there, sitting and crying."

Raymond Ford, twenty-two and an African-American, was the first soldier from tiny Bardstown, Kentucky, to die in the Vietnam War. Sadly, he was not the last. As luck would have it, Bardstown lost more than its share of men in Vietnam. Several left children behind.

Ellen Crawford never got to see her father, James J. Crawford, who died in Vietnam. Ellen's mother, Rebecca, says Ellen is bitter about not having the chance to know and love her dad. "This important part of her life is missing," Rebecca Crawford says. Rebecca worries that, if the war was as bad as people say, Ellen will wonder why her father was involved. "I want her to feel that her daddy was doing a good job."

Although most Americans today realize that the men and women who served in Vietnam did a good job, they also are aware that the war was a tragedy that damaged the nation. To understand how good people can get involved in a bad war, it is necessary to study a lengthy chain of events leading to the conflict.

Vietnam, halfway around the world in Southeast Asia, was originally divided into North Vietnam and South Vietnam in 1954, before the United States' involvement. North Vietnam was ruled by communists, South Vietnam by noncommunists. Many Vietnamese on both sides of the dividing line wanted one country, but they disagreed violently on who should run the nation and what form of government it should have.

Because the United States wanted to stop the spread of communism from North to South Vietnam, it propped up the South. All across South Vietnam, U.S. soldiers and Army of the Republic of Vietnam (ARVN) troops fought communist Vietcong guerrillas and North Vietnamese Army (NVA) members. In part because soldiers from the North were fighting in

His skin smeared with camouflage, this young American soldier shows the strain of battle. The average U.S. serviceman was seven years younger than his World War II counterpart.

the South, U.S. planes dropped hundreds of thousands of bombs on North Vietnam's villages, cities, and supply lines.

The Vietnam War was the longest conflict in the history of the United States. The first U.S. ground troops landed in Vietnam in 1965; the last American forces departed in 1973. Two years after U.S. withdrawal, North Vietnamese soldiers swept across all of South Vietnam. Did the United States pull out after realizing that it had, in effect, lost the war?

Some Americans would say yes: Despite the sacrifice of people, weapons, and billions of dollars, communism engulfed Vietnam. Others think the answer is no: They argue that the U.S. withdrawal merely shifted responsibility for fighting the war to the South Vietnamese. Still others feel the outcome was neither a win nor a loss because the conflict was a civil war between two sides of a divided country.

The Cost of War

The war was a terrible one. It cost the lives of more than fifty-eight thousand Americans, most of them very young. The average age of the American soldier in Vietnam was nineteen, seven years younger than the average GI in World War II. All of them were sons and many were fathers or brothers. For more years than younger Americans could remember, the dead returned on military flights through Oakland, California, in shiny alu-

minum coffins, headed to funeral homes for military burial in cities and towns all over the country.

The conflict hit some parts of the U.S. population harder than others. African-American and Latino men were overrepresented in the Vietnam War and became overrepresented in the list of individuals who died. Most of the soldiers came from poor or working-class families, and few of them were educated beyond high school, as college deferments would have kept students from being drafted.

Above: The returned remains of an American soldier are saluted in Hanoi in 1992. *Below:* U.S. nurse Karen Walters works to save the lives of children injured when American jets bombed a village in 1966.

Not all of those who returned to the United States considered themselves lucky. Some had walked into antipersonnel mines or were burned by napalm (jellied-gasoline) bombs or suffered gunshot or shrapnel wounds. They came home missing limbs or with painful or disfiguring injuries. Nor were all of those who served in Southeast Asia men. Some seventy-five hundred female nurses spent twelve-hour days caring for wounded soldiers.

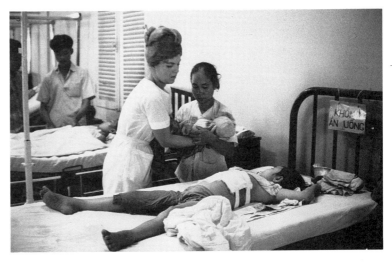

A marine is carried to a helicopter, which will transport him from a field hospital in Da Nang, South Vietnam, to a U.S. hospital ship. The photo was taken in December 1967 as U.S. Marines defended remote firebases near the demilitarized zone (DMZ).

A total of 365,000 soldiers were wounded, 14,000 of them seriously. Some continue to suffer today from skin diseases or forms of cancer they believe were caused by Agent Orange. This chemical herbicide, named for its orange containers, was sprayed by plane on thick jungles to kill vegetation that hid the enemy. Veterans feel that exposure to Agent Orange and other toxic substances has disabled them or their children or played a part in their illnesses and deaths. Chemical companies that made the substance settled a 1984 lawsuit out of court for $180 million. The money went to aid those who claimed they and their offspring had been hurt by Agent Orange.

Most of the 2.1 million people who served in Vietnam returned home without wounds and readjusted to civilian life. But others carried deep emotional scars. These veterans have trouble sleeping — they are haunted by nightmares, or they suffer flashbacks that delude them into thinking they are still in peril on a distant battlefield. Others returned addicted to costly drugs that destroyed their lives.

For all the suffering of American veterans, the Vietnamese suffered more. Two million Vietnamese died, and four million were wounded. More than ten million people, most of them civilians, lost their homes. Some five million acres of forest and cropland were ruined by eighteen million gallons of chemical poisons. Bombs and artillery erased many villages and damaged numerous cities. Vietnam's water still bubbles with potent and dangerous petroleum and other chemicals.

Vietnamese women fill sandbags near the village of Ben Het in 1969. Sandbags served as protection against mortars — shells fired from a portable tube that exploded on impact, blowing jagged metal over a wide area.

This Vietnamese boy, a resident of Ben Het, survived a communist siege of the small camp where he lived. Civilians often found themselves caught in the crossfire of war.

A Country Divided

The Vietnam War split America apart almost as surely as if it had been fought on U.S. soil. Many people openly and bitterly disagreed on whether America should have sent troops to fight in Vietnam, especially as the fighting widened and became more intense. Some said the United States had no valid reason to be in Vietnam; they believed America was interfering with the right of the Vietnamese to choose their government and leaders, even if that choice led to communist rule of the entire country.

Other Americans felt that fighting communism in Vietnam was an important and honorable goal that deserved military and public support. They were convinced that fighting communism in Vietnam was preferable to fighting communism as it spread to Hawaii or the U.S. West Coast. Communism, some said, should be fought wherever it attempted to expand, in Asia and elsewhere. This is the concept of containment, developed by high-ranking State Department official George Kennan in the 1940s and advocated in the early 1950s by people such as John Foster Dulles, U.S. secretary of state under President Dwight D. Eisenhower.

A draft resister burns his orders to report for the military in front of his father and friends in New York City on the morning of January 29, 1968. Antiwar protests became larger and more frequent as the war ground on.

Many of the young men who were eligible to serve in the war were afraid to go. They knew that if they went, they probably would have to kill people or be killed themselves. Their families were frightened, as well. To avoid the war, some men fled to Canada. They headed north, not knowing if they would ever be readmitted to the United States. Other young men were so afraid of going to Vietnam that they physically hurt themselves to avoid being drafted.

To this day, some adults are unable to speak of the Vietnam War. Such an emotional attitude makes it difficult for young people to learn about U.S. involvement, especially because involvement began long before today's young people were born.

A Small, Strategic Land

Vietnam was occupied for centuries by one foreign power and then another. One reason for foreign occupation was the country's geography, a subject few Americans knew much about. The country is in Southeast Asia on the western edge of the Pacific Ocean. Some eight thousand miles west of Los Angeles, it is bordered by China on the north, Laos on the west, and Cambodia on the southwest. The eastern side of the country is a body of water called the South China Sea. The northeast coast is defined by the Gulf of Tonkin. With 127,242 square miles, the country is about the size of the state of New Mexico.

This 1966 map shows the countries that made up Southeast Asia at the time of the war in Vietnam: North Vietnam, South Vietnam, Laos, and Cambodia. China has always been a strong influence in Southeast Asia.

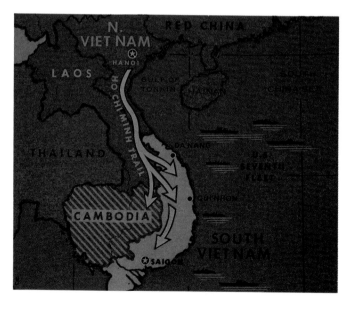

Vietnamese say the country looks like two fat rice baskets on either end of a long, thin pole. The pole is the Annamese Mountain chain, which runs from one end of the country to the other. The rice baskets are flat, fertile river deltas. The Red River is in the North and the Mekong River is in the South. Both areas grow huge amounts of rice, more than the Vietnamese can eat in those years when the harvest is plentiful. Vietnam also is rich in tin, tungsten, coal, and oil, and rubber trees grow in the southern part of the country, just above the Mekong Delta.

Located along the sea route between the mighty civilizations of India and China, Vietnam was easy to find. China moved into the country in 221 B.C., ruling it for more than one thousand years. The Vietnamese absorbed many Chinese customs, yet they smoldered with resentment under foreign rule and threw the Chinese out in A.D. 939. For more than eight hundred years, the Vietnamese enjoyed independence. They adopted the Chinese customs they liked and cultivated traditions of their own, mixing the religion of Buddhism with ancestor worship and with the teachings of Confucius, a Chinese philosopher.

European traders arrived in Vietnam in the sixteenth century. They were followed a century later by Roman Catholic missionaries, most of them French. The missionaries converted millions of Vietnamese to Christianity before a Vietnamese emperor, Minh Mang, decided in 1825 not to admit additional missionaries. That did little good, so in 1833, Minh ordered his troops to arrest Catholic priests, whom he considered meddlers. The Vietnamese executed ten of the French priests, which proved to be a mistake.

Vietnamese laborers use rice baskets to transport sand along the Red River near Hanoi, North Vietnam. Both Vietnams depended on rivers for the health of the rice crop.

If the French were looking for an excuse to invade Vietnam, the deaths of the priests provided it. France may have been angered by the killings, but it was also concerned about something else entirely — Great Britain, Germany, the Netherlands, Portugal, and Spain all seemed to have a larger and more profitable string of colonies, and France wanted to expand its holdings. The French felt that the Vietnamese would be a large new market for French-made goods.

France Takes Control

When the French moved into Vietnam in 1858, 80 percent of the Vietnamese were literate. When they left in 1954, 80 percent of the Vietnamese were unable to read or write. The French damaged the country and its people not by constant physical cruelty but by humiliation — they told the Vietnamese that they were inferior — and division — they kept them separated. To prevent any kind of national unity, they divided the country into three parts: the north was called Tonkin, the center Annam, and the south Cochinchina. These three countries, plus Laos and Cambodia, became what was known as French Indochina.

By overseeing the government and by owning all land, business, and industry, the French remained in complete control throughout their colonial rule. This control made many French citizens wealthy at the expense of most Vietnamese, who became increasingly poor. This poverty resulted from the French buying land away from Vietnamese peasants at a price that

French soldiers, in the foreground, prepare to depart as Vietminh troops (followers of Ho Chi Minh) move into Haiphong, North Vietnam's big port, in 1955. Under terms of an agreement made in 1954 in Geneva, Switzerland, Vietnam was split between communist north and noncommunist south.

would not support the peasant family for very long. The former owners became laborers in mines or on rubber plantations, or they farmed as tenants.

As tenant farmers, the Vietnamese had to pay rents equal to about half of the profit from the sale of their rice harvest. When harvests were poor, the tenants had to borrow money from the French to prevent starvation. This indebted them and prevented them from moving to other opportunities. One reason for the drop in literacy was that school-age children were forced to work in the fields to help the family rather than attend classes.

Those who fared best under French rule were members of the small, educated Vietnamese middle class. They were Roman Catholic and most often lived in southern Vietnam, where land was plentiful and the rice harvests were usually the largest. Others were appointed to midlevel government jobs, though they were paid less than their French counterparts. Some were taught French from birth and never learned to speak or write Vietnamese.

Many Vietnamese, especially the landless peasants, regarded the French as intruders during their century of rule. Years of humiliation and injustice, coupled with the desire to unify Vietnam, led people to work secretly for independence. They were inspired by an emerging revolutionary leader who lived in northern Vietnam. This son of a schoolteacher called himself Ho Chi Minh.

Ho wanted to throw the French out and then make sure that land and other resources were shared equally by all Vietnamese. He believed that a communist government would best distribute the resources. (Under communism, a one-party government controls the economy, usually deciding that land and other goods must be shared.) Communism appealed to many peasants, but it frightened middle- and upper-class Vietnamese, who feared losing their possessions and being deprived of their Christian religion.

Ho Chi Minh's followers became known as the Vietminh. Because the primary goal of the Vietminh was independence, they attracted nationalists — people who wanted a free Vietnam. Some of the patriots believed that a communist government should replace French rule, whereas others simply wanted the Viet-

Ho Chi Minh and communism

The son of a Vietnamese teacher and government official who resigned to protest French rule, Ho Chi Minh grew up hearing stories about Vietnamese heroes. Ho acquired a sense of adventure, taking a job on a French ocean liner that carried him to many ports all over the world. He lived briefly in New York City, where he came to admire Americans and their strong sense of independence. Toward the end of World War I, at the age of about twenty-eight, the globetrotter settled in Paris.

When U.S. President Woodrow Wilson arrived in Paris in 1919 to attend the Versailles conference that would formally end World War I, Ho handed him a petition. The paper asked Allied leaders to liberate Vietnam from French rule. Although Wilson and other conference members ignored Ho's plea for self-rule, another group, the French Socialist Party, was quite impressed. With other socialists, Ho helped form the French Communist Party.

Communist leaders in the new Soviet Union invited Ho to Moscow, where he learned more about communism and grew to believe that this economic system and form of government could help Vietnam achieve independence. From there, Ho moved to southern China and then to northern Vietnam. In 1941, he organized the first communist force in Vietnam, the Vietminh.

Ho owned little or no property, never married, and lived in caves and in other crude dwellings for several years while rallying his people during World War II. His wisdom, warm personality, and long life attracted many followers, who called him Uncle Ho. But in 1955, Ho gained a reputation for ruthlessness when his land reforms caused landless peasants to kill some ten thousand small farmers. Their only sin had been property ownership. Ho stopped the land-reform program in 1956, publicly apologizing for the needless killing.

French forces celebrate a holiday with a military parade in the early 1950s in Hanoi, North Vietnam. Despite having superior weapons, the French were defeated by the Vietminh's hit-and-run guerrilla tactics.

namese to rule themselves. World War II gave this ragged band of activists their chance.

World War II

World War II marked another kind of foreign occupation for the Vietnamese. This time, the invaders were fellow Asians — the Japanese. Troops from Japan arrived in Vietnam in 1940, pushing the French out of power. When it appeared obvious in 1945 that the Japanese would lose the war, Ho Chi Minh and his followers decided the time was right for Vietnam to declare its independence. On September 2, 1945, Ho entered the northern city of Hanoi and declared Vietnam an independent nation.

Unfortunately, no one paid any attention to this declaration. Immediately following the end of the war, the United States and its allies asked China and Great Britain to position troops in Vietnam to keep the peace. Ho knew the British would not stay for long because Britain was more concerned about rebuilding its bombed cities and weakened economy. But the Chinese presence concerned him because the huge, overpopulated nation lay just to the north of his own small country.

To encourage the Chinese to leave, Ho Chi Minh invited the French to take their place. Weary from fighting in World War II, the Chinese agreed to the plan — but not before hungry Chinese soldiers devoured virtually all of Vietnam's stored food. Some of Ho's followers deserted him for appealing to the French, but Ho insisted that the Chinese might be worse. The French agreed to respect Vietnam's independence on their return, but it became clear shortly after their arrival that their promise was an empty one.

War with France

Following an argument over tax payments in 1946, the French ignited a war. They fired shells from a ship in a harbor off the northern coastal city of Haiphong while dropping bombs on the big port from the air. When the attack ended, six thousand Vietnamese civilians lay dead and several neighborhoods were destroyed. The civilian population rioted, and fighting between the French and Vietnamese spread. At that point, Ho Chi Minh asked the United States for help.

President Franklin D. Roosevelt considered giving Ho Chi Minh financial aid, in part because Ho's Vietminh volunteers rescued several downed American flyers and worked with the U.S. Office of Strategic Services (today's Central Intelligence Agency) during World War II. Roosevelt also disliked France's colonialism and the country's leader, Charles de Gaulle. But President Harry S. Truman, Roosevelt's successor, refused Ho's plea.

Truman was under pressure, from Democrats and Republicans alike, not to support anyone who might have been a communist.

That attitude was one result of the tension between the United States and the Soviet Union. It would lead to a long and costly war of words and sword rattling that historians would call the Cold War. After 1945, many U.S. decision makers believed the Soviet Union was determined to rule the world. Because both Soviet leader Joseph Stalin and Ho Chi Minh were communists, the Americans suspected that Ho was under orders from Stalin.

Meanwhile, the Vietminh gathered a meager supply of weapons and started a hit-and-run war with the French that lasted eight years. As this Indochinese War became more intense, so did American fear of communism. There were several reasons for such fear: China, the world's most populous country, had adopted communism in 1949. Plus, communist North Korea attacked South Korea in 1950. And, as Great Britain's Winston Churchill pointed out, an "iron curtain" of communist rule had fallen across most of Eastern Europe.

The response by the United States, Great Britain, and their allies was a series of pacts and alliances such as the North Atlantic Treaty Organization (NATO). But the United States went further. Truman, Secretary of State Dean Acheson, and others decided on a policy of communist containment.

President Dwight D. Eisenhower refused to aid the French in Vietnam in 1954 because he disliked the prospect of a land war involving U.S. forces in Asia.

This meant that noncommunist governments would be given aid so they would not accept support from the Soviet Union. Aid in the form of food, weapons, and technology would prevent the spread of communism, U.S. leaders reasoned.

To contain communism in Southeast Asia, the United States backed the French in their struggles with the Vietminh. If, as some historians believe, Truman was blind to the evils of a European power using a country as a colony, so were others during the Cold War. Anticommunism in the United States was as deeply felt as religious beliefs. Many people were convinced that, if the United States failed to stop the communist menace anywhere on earth, it would soon appear at America's door.

After years of losing people in ambushes and in small but vicious battles, the French moved hundreds of troops into a remote mountain valley in northern Vietnam called Dien Bien Phu. Although this was a crossroads for the Vietminh as they moved out of the mountains and into the more populated areas of Vietnam, it was a terrible decision by the French. For fifty-five days, the surrounded and outnumbered French troops suffered horrible losses as Vietminh gunners rained artillery down on the soldiers and edged close enough to pick them off with mortars and machine-gun or rifle fire. Repeatedly, the French asked President Dwight D. Eisenhower for air strikes against the enemy, but the United States refused.

The French Depart

Eisenhower and such Democrats as Senator Lyndon B. Johnson were, by 1954, sick of war. They had battled to a draw in Korea, and the president was fond of saying he did not want to wage a war on the Asian mainland. Equally important, Eisenhower had been elected in 1952 on a promise to end fighting in Korea, not to begin another war. French forces surrendered to troops under North Vietnam's General Vo Nguyen Giap, a former schoolteacher, on May 7, 1954. France slowly began to pull soldiers and civilians out of what had been French Indochina.

That same year, leaders met half a world away in Geneva, Switzerland. This peace conference was called the Geneva Convention, and it was decided there that the best way to separate communists from noncommunists in Vietnam was to divide the country into two roughly equal parts. A demilitarized zone separated the two new countries, which were called North Vietnam and South Vietnam. While Ho Chi Minh and his followers migrated to or remained in the North, Roman Catholics and other people with property moved to or remained in the South. A national election set for 1956 would decide who should lead a single, reunited Vietnam.

Elections and Their Results

Ho Chi Minh's popularity certainly made him the leading candidate. In comparison, Bao Dai, the figurehead emperor kept in power by the French, was an unpopular playboy. He appointed a little-known anticommunist named Ngo Dinh Diem as prime minister of South Vietnam. Diem looked like an attractive candidate to the United States. To improve Diem's chances, the United States began to aid South Vietnam. American involvement included providing food, money, and mostly agricultural technology, but it also included U.S. Air Force mechanics assigned to keeping South Vietnam's aircraft flying.

Soon after becoming the South's prime minister, Diem decided he wanted to be South Vietnam's president. He won a rigged election, which he would have probably won anyway, and pledged to stand against the communist tide. There were few communists in the South at the time because the Vietminh had either moved into North Vietnam or retreated into the mountains that run along Vietnam's border with Laos. As the French pulled out, Emperor Bao Dai moved to France and decided to remain in Europe.

Communist groups in the South were weak and without many weapons or much leadership. They and others opposed to Diem formed the National Liberation Front, whose members became known as the Vietcong. Diem convinced himself that all who were opposed to him must be communists. He attacked everyone from rural religious sects to gangs operating on the Saigon docks, looking the other way as police and the military arrested, tortured, or killed innocent citizens. The Vietcong looked northward for leadership and found it in Ho Chi Minh.

Ho and his advisors taught the Vietcong to retaliate by killing South Vietnamese village chiefs and other officials who supported Diem. Both Diem and the United States ignored the 1956 deadline for the national election, so Ho realized he would never peacefully rule a united Vietnam, despite his popularity. To stop Vietcong assassinations, and to keep noncommunists such as the Buddhists in line, Diem and his followers decided that they should have larger and better-trained armed forces.

Colored smoke sends a coded signal to a helicopter, telling the pilot where to drop food and weapons at a U.S. Green Beret camp in the central highlands of Vietnam. The camp was under siege by communist forces for fifty-six days in 1969.

Kennedy's Cold Warriors

President John F. Kennedy came to office in 1961 after narrowly defeating Richard M. Nixon in the 1960 election. His advisors argued about what to do in Vietnam, with Secretary of State Dean Rusk getting the upper hand. Rusk, a lifelong anticommunist, convinced listeners that Ho Chi Minh's efforts to unify Vietnam were part of a Soviet plan to extend communism across all of Southeast Asia. To contain the threat, he said, the South Vietnamese must be aggressive. Secretary of Defense Robert S. McNamara agreed. The question was, what role should the United States play?

Kennedy believed a better, larger South Vietnamese army would help, but that army would be of little use unless it learned to stop a guerrilla war. Seven hundred of the U.S. Army's antiguerrilla Special Forces (or Green Berets) had been sent by former President Eisenhower as military advisors to aid South Vietnam, and they had helped create the Army of the Republic of Vietnam (ARVN). Kennedy sent nearly one hundred more advisors early in 1961 and, by the end of 1962, had moved about nine thousand Americans into South Vietnam. Although the U.S. public did not know it, some "advisors" had secretly been involved in combat.

Military advisors did little to improve the Diem regime, which was riddled with corruption. Equally important, the appearance of U.S. troops riled the Vietcong, who began to receive more and better weapons and supplies from the North. Diem himself became less and less effective, relying on the advice of his unstable, drug-addicted brother, Ngo Dinh Nhu, and the brother's wife, Madame Nhu. U.S. advisors were told by military men that they planned to overthrow their president. U.S. personnel indicated they would not oppose such a move.

Madame Nhu, sister-in-law of Prime Minister Ngo Dinh Diem, was French educated and learned to speak Vietnamese but never learned to write it. She and her husband influenced South Vietnamese policy in the early 1960s.

Diem and his brother were shot to death by army officers on November 1, 1963, but their deaths were overshadowed in the United States by the assassination of John F. Kennedy three weeks later. At the time of Kennedy's death, 16,300 Americans, mostly soldiers, were in Vietnam, and more than 100 Americans, most of them soldiers, had been killed. Vice President Lyndon B. Johnson, who had helped deny the French airpower at Dien Bien Phu in 1954, was sworn in following Kennedy's death.

Gaining confidence with each day in office, President Johnson had widespread support because the presidency was unexpectedly thrust upon him. His popularity increased as he declared war on poverty, vowed to fight segregation and other social ills, and improved a shaky economy. Lyndon Johnson believed he could solve the problems that beset Vietnam while leading the United States to greatness at home. He won a landslide victory in the 1964 presidential election, in part because he portrayed his opponent, Barry Goldwater, as someone who wanted to recklessly use nuclear weapons. With at least four years left to serve, Johnson looked confidently across the Pacific toward Vietnam.

Members of the U.S. Army's 101 Airborne Division in 1968 honor members who were killed in Vietnam during their tour. Marines were required to serve thirteen months in Vietnam, whereas all other branches served for one year.

CHAPTER TWO

Escalation: The Human Cost

Despite his misgivings, President Johnson broadened, or escalated, the Vietnam War after taking office in late 1963. Johnson's actions were based on commitments of previous presidents, and he, too, would make commitments that future presidents felt they had to honor. At the time, he was also concerned that the government of South Vietnam had become less able to confront the growth and strength of the Vietcong. A number of his advisors and members of Congress advocated more U.S. participation in Vietnam.

Whereas Johnson had concerns about the government, American military advisors had serious doubts about the ability of the Army of the Republic of Vietnam (ARVN) as early as January 1963 — and with good reason. At the tiny village of Ap Bac, forty miles southwest of Saigon, a much smaller force of disciplined Vietcong guerrillas battered a South Vietnamese force of as many as fifteen thousand men. The Vietcong attacked viciously and then disappeared in thick, lowlying vegetation when ARVN troops belatedly counterattacked. The U.S. media reported this disaster, which probably was caused by indecision on the part of South Vietnamese military officers.

The assassinated President Diem of South Vietnam was replaced by a general, Nguyen Khan, but the general was unable to rule effectively. Taking advantage of South Vietnam's lack of leadership, Ho Chi Minh directed the Vietcong to intensify their efforts. Using threats of violence or physical harm, the Vietcong recruited peasant farmers and persuaded others to donate food and supplies to the rebel cause. Other peasants, disgusted with their corrupt and inefficient government, willingly joined the Vietcong. They thought a revolution might be a good thing.

Strangers in South Vietnam

As Lyndon Johnson was taking the oath of office aboard Air Force One in November, almost ten thousand North Vietnamese Army (NVA) troops were sent south along the Ho Chi Minh trail to join and aid the Vietcong.

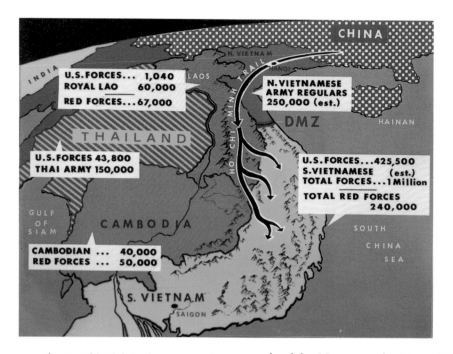

The map labels read:

CHINA

N. VIETNAM

U.S. FORCES... 1,040
ROYAL LAO 60,000
RED FORCES... 67,000

INDIA

LAOS

N. VIETNAMESE
ARMY REGULARS
250,000 (est.)

DMZ

HAINAN

THAILAND

U.S. FORCES 43,800
THAI ARMY 150,000

U.S. FORCES... 425,500
S. VIETNAMESE (est.)
TOTAL FORCES... 1 Million
TOTAL RED FORCES
240,000

GULF
OF
SIAM

CAMBODIA

SOUTH
CHINA
SEA

CAMBODIAN ... 40,000
RED FORCES ... 50,000

S. VIETNAM
SAIGON

HO CHI MINH TRAIL

The Ho Chi Minh trail snakes out of North Vietnam and winds through portions of Laos and Cambodia. The trail fed troops and supplies into South Vietnam for years, despite U.S. and South Vietnamese efforts to stem the flow.

The trail was a network of paths that began in the highlands of North Vietnam and led through remote areas of Laos and Cambodia, ending in South Vietnam. North Vietnamese troops no older than their American counterparts braved bad weather, rough terrain, malaria, tuberculosis, and other diseases to reach the South. Soon, they would have to cringe in the jungle as U.S. airpower pounded the Ho Chi Minh trail day and night.

In response to the growing strength of the Vietcong, the United States sent more aid to South Vietnam. By March of 1964, the number of U.S. advisors totaled 23,300. Although these advisors still were not supposed to engage in combat, many did. Saigon, the South Vietnamese capital, became an outpost for American government workers, soldiers, and journalists. These people were among the victims of Vietcong terrorist bombs detonated in bars, restaurants, and other American hangouts. But it took an incident in the Gulf of Tonkin, off the coast of North Vietnam, for the United States to become openly involved in fighting communist aggression.

On August 2, 1964, small South Vietnamese patrol torpedo (PT) boats attacked North Vietnamese naval bases on islands in the Gulf of Tonkin. During the attacks, a U.S. destroyer named the *Maddox* was nearby. The *Maddox* was equipped with electronic surveillance equipment to spy on the North Vietnamese bases. After the PT attacks, the North Vietnamese assumed the *Maddox* was involved, and they sent three of their own PT boats in pursuit of the U.S. craft. The North Vietnamese fired a torpedo that missed, and the *Maddox* sank one PT boat and badly damaged the other two.

The commander of the *Maddox* and the commander of another nearby destroyer, the *C. Turner Joy*, expected more trouble and notified President Johnson. Johnson moved U.S. planes and pilots into South Vietnam and placed stateside combat troops on alert. Two days later, on August 4, the *Maddox* commander radioed Washington that his vessel was about to be torpedoed. It turned out that he was wrong, but the report prompted quick and aggressive action. U.S. warplanes dropped bombs on North Vietnamese naval stations and on twenty-five PT boats. Two U.S. planes were shot down in the raid, with one pilot captured and one missing.

The Gulf of Tonkin Resolution

Johnson was quickly convinced that U. S. combat forces would be needed, but he did not want to act without Congress. His aides drew up a document called the Gulf of Tonkin Resolution, which was presented to Congress for its approval. The resolution gave the president the power to take "all necessary measures to repel any armed attack against the forces of the United States and to prevent further aggression" in Southeast Asia. The resolution passed the House by 416 to 0 and the Senate by 88 to 2 on August 7. The bill was "like grandma's nightshirt," President Johnson later said, "it covered everything."

Although the president could now wage war on North Vietnam, he was still uncertain how to go about it. As South Vietnamese political leaders served badly and briefly, Johnson's advisors argued about what action the president should take. William Bundy, assistant secretary of state for Far Eastern affairs, along with the nation's military leaders, recommended regular bombing of North Vietnam's bridges, railroads, and oil-storage facilities. A member of the U.S. State Department, Walter Rostow, urged bombing plus sending troops immediately.

Maxwell Taylor, the ambassador to South Vietnam and a former U.S. Army general, was against bombing the North. He and others believed such an action would lead to stepped-up Vietcong attacks on inexperienced Army of the Republic of Vietnam (ARVN) units. That, in turn, would lead to U.S. troops engaging in actual combat on behalf of the South Vietnamese. Taylor feared a never-ending ground war that would eventually pull in China and the Soviet Union on the Vietcong side.

For six months, the president refrained from sending more planes or troops to Vietnam. But on February 7, 1965, Vietcong units attacked an American base at Pleiku in South Vietnam's central highlands. The base housed Marines, and the attack killed several as they slept in their bunks. President Johnson took immediate action, ordering the bombing of North Vietnam. The air war, called "Rolling Thunder," began March 2, 1965, and lasted three years. It would increase in intensity with each passing month.

On March 8, 1965, the first U.S. ground forces specifically sent to fight

Army of the Republic of Vietnam (ARVN) troops stop to eat field rations during an operation. ARVN units frequently were inexperienced and their leaders corrupt.

A weapons mechanic at Da Nang, South Vietnam, installs fins on air-to-air missiles that will be carried by the U.S. Air Force F-4C Phantom jets in the background. The North Vietnamese had few aircraft but were supplied by allies with deadly ground-to-air missiles.

landed in Vietnam. These were thirty-five hundred Marines, assigned to keep the big air base at Da Nang safe from enemy attack. The base was a prime target for Vietcong mortars because every plane that was damaged on the ground was one less plane capable of attacking the North. Marine patrols probed in a radius of several miles around the base, with mixed results. By August, however, members of the corps had staged the first big U.S. ground operation of the war, crippling a large Vietcong unit and making the air base safe to use round-the-clock.

Lessons from the Ia Drang Valley

Two months later, with the number of American service personnel in Vietnam nearing two hundred thousand, one of the most important battles of the war took place. An army airborne division, using helicopters to move troops in and out of combat, defeated three regiments of North Vietnamese soldiers in the remote Ia Drang valley. The victory prevented the NVA from sweeping out of the central highlands to the coast. It also answered several nagging questions.

Among the most important questions was whether airmobile army units, relying on helicopters and using air and artillery support, would be an effective fighting force in Vietnam. The answer certainly appeared to be yes. Would the huge B-52 bombers be of any use to support ground forces? That answer was yes, too, as the huge aircraft repeatedly bombed the enemy while it lay in wait for arriving U.S. ground troops. Regarding North Vietnam, would NVA soldiers stand up to the better-equipped Americans? The North Vietnamese fought with great courage, suffering huge losses.

Some three hundred Americans and two thousand North Vietnamese lost their lives in the battle, which lasted for about two weeks. The search-

Military versus media

The United States armed forces and the U.S. media grew to despise each other during the Vietnam War. The intense dislike stemmed in part from the fact that neither knew much about the other. The military's job was to carry out the orders of the commander-in-chief, whereas radio, television, and newspaper people were told to find out what was happening in Vietnam and report it to the people back home.

From the start, the relationship was awkward at best. Military leaders spoke of matters euphemistically — they used bland, deceptive language in place of blunt, accurate words. "Target-rich environment" might really mean there were many human beings in an area to be bombed. "Harassment and interdiction" artillery fire sounded impressive but really was intended to separate flesh from bone as it disrupted and terrorized the enemy. The more probing the questions asked by the news media, the more a member of the military was apt to use such deceptive language.

On the other hand, military people failed to realize that a soldier doing a good job was not much of a story. The media looked for dope users, enemy gains, corruption, and mutinies and other conflicts between officers and soldiers. Because the Vietnam War was becoming more unpopular every week, it was easy to find discontent and defeat in the ranks of U.S. service personnel.

U.S. forces held a daily news conference that took place in Saigon. A military spokesperson would tell what had happened during the previous twenty-four hours and would attempt to answer questions from the media. This worked well enough until some reporters went out into the field. There, they saw that the daily news conferences were utter lies — the South Vietnamese were inept soldiers, and the Vietcong and the North Vietnamese were brave and resourceful. The daily news briefings, held every afternoon, became known as "The Five O'Clock Follies."

Even more convincing than the words that reached the United States were the pictures. Motion picture film could be shot one day and beamed into living rooms via television the next. The evening news frequently ruined suppers by showing bloody, vicious fighting, much of it involving soldiers who looked like neighborhood kids. Still photographers seemed to be everywhere, transmitting wire-service photos of Vietnamese children burned by napalm or the close-range execution of a prisoner of war by a South Vietnamese military man. It is no exaggeration to state that the words and pictures coming out of Vietnam strongly influenced public opinion.

and-destroy operation led General William Westmoreland, head of the military in Vietnam, to report that the United States would grind the enemy down by continuing to have favorable "kill ratios," that is, more North Vietnamese dead than American or ARVN soldiers killed. Westmoreland failed to realize that the Vietnamese were prepared to suffer huge losses for as long as it might take to win the war. He also did not realize that trading the lives of Americans for the lives of Vietnamese would turn much of the U.S. civilian population against the war.

Human Statistics

Two young people, one American and one Vietnamese, entirely unknown to each other, would become part of the Vietnam War era in June of 1966. Mike, from Erie, Pennsylvania, was a recent college graduate. The form in the mail ordered him to take a physical examination to determine if he

Two wounded U.S. military advisors await evacuation from Lai Khe following fighting in 1972. Helicopter pilots often braved heavy fire to dart in and pick up wounded soldiers.

should be drafted into the U.S. Army. The twenty-two-year-old had met with a Marine recruiter earlier, while at college. The recruiter told Mike he would make a good officer and should consider enlisting in the Marine Corps when he received the physical exam notice. Mike took the recruiter's advice.

Across the globe, a woman named Nguyen joined the cluster of people around a stranger in her village in North Vietnam. The stranger spoke through an old megaphone, telling villagers to prepare for bombing by U.S. planes. He told them to construct bunkers, and he said antiaircraft guns would be arriving from Haiphong so that residents could shoot at attacking planes. "Don't assume your village is too small to be hit," the government official warned. Nguyen and others immediately dug a trench on one side of the village while others fortified the area with wooden spikes and camouflage.

Neither Mike nor Nguyen would survive the war. Mike, thoughtful and athletic, became a U.S. Marine Corps second lieutenant. He died in 1967 in South Vietnam after only six weeks in combat. Defending an artillery base, Mike was hit by shrapnel during a night attack by an NVA unit. Nguyen, known as a good mother with a sweet voice, died the same year, killed by bomb fragments as she ran toward the trench she had helped dig. Today, except among families and friends, Mike and Nguyen are remembered only as statistics.

Those statistics are staggering. Of the 8.7 million Americans who served during the period January 1, 1961, to September 30, 1977, a total of 58,151 soldiers were killed. Some 153,303 suffered various wounds and injuries. By comparison, the Vietnamese were much worse off: North Vietnam lost as many as 900,000 soldiers, South Vietnam more than 200,000, and more than one million civilians lost their lives. Wounds and injuries were so common that in every village among the country's 70 million people today, there are amputees and residents with disfiguring scars. So many North Vietnamese Army members died that a popular NVA tattoo read, "Born in the North, die in the South."

The dying did not necessarily end in 1975 with the reunification of the two Vietnams. After the war, Vietnamese clearing remote areas so that they might plant crops sometimes set off mines that killed or maimed them. U.S. veterans and Vietnamese veterans and civilians experienced a number of birth defects among their children and an increased number of cancers from exposure to defoliants and other harsh chemicals. They also suffered various skin maladies. People on both sides strongly suspected herbicides, particularly Agent Orange, as the cause. These chemical agents were sprayed from U.S. airplanes to thin out thick, enemy-infested forests. Only recently has the U.S. government begun treating veterans who say they were damaged from chemical exposure.

A U.S. Army medic works on the wound of a fellow soldier. The most common wounds were caused by shrapnel — bits of sharp metal that flew through the air following the explosion of an artillery or mortar shell, or a rocket or grenade.

Who Fought for America?

Mike was not a typical soldier. He was slightly older and better educated. Because he was a college graduate, he served as an officer. (Most Vietnam veterans served not as officers but as privates, corporals, specialists, and sergeants.) The average American trooper in Vietnam was only nineteen years old, with a high school diploma or less, from a working-class family. All young men were required to register for the draft at a local Selective Service System office immediately following their eighteenth birthday. Each was given a draft card that, by federal law, he had to carry with him at all times. If the potential draftee did not get a deferment (delay) to attend college or because he was married and had a child, he could — and probably would — be drafted some time after his nineteenth birthday.

Eighteen-year-olds were classified I-A, which meant they could be ordered to undergo a physical exam to determine fitness for military service. College students were classified II-S, which indicated they would be allowed to complete their current year of college and could renew the II-S classification each year they enrolled as full-time students. Persons who had criminal records, flunked the physical exam, or had a history of drug use, homosexuality, or mental problems were classified IV-F and were not accepted. Young men who flunked an intelligence test, given at the time of the physical, were also ineligible to serve.

Those who opposed the war for religious reasons were termed conscientious objectors; the difficulty of obtaining this status varied from draft board to draft board. Conscientious objectors were sometimes allowed to work in hospitals or perform other kinds of nonmilitary service. Religious beliefs that qualified men for conscientious objector status included Quakers (Society of Friends) and Seventh-Day Adventists, among others. Some pacifists allowed themselves to be inducted and participated in training, but they refused to use weapons. Often, they served in uniform in a hospital in the United States, in Vietnam, or elsewhere.

Young Americans are inducted into the military in 1968. The vast majority of men went into the U.S. Army, but a few were drafted into the U.S. Marines.

Draft offices numbered about eight thousand and were located in cities and in county seats across the country. Their boards, which decided whom to draft, were made up of local residents. Draft boards called all eligible men twenty-six years of age and younger, taking the oldest first. In wealthy areas with few young adult males not attending college, nineteen-year-olds

were called almost immediately following their birthdays. To reduce the possibility of ending up in combat, many young men enlisted, joining the service and agreeing to serve for longer periods of time in exchange for noncombat military jobs. It was commonly known that the army and the marines did most of the close-in fighting, with the air force and the navy providing support. Consequently, navy and air force staffing were easily filled. The National Guard, too, provided some escape from combat.

Just as there was a draft board in most cities, there were military recruiters with quotas to fill, too. These people obtained lists of men about to be drafted and tried to steer them into their own branch of the service. The air force, Coast Guard, and navy easily met their quotas, whereas the army and the marines had difficulty finding enough men. Those who were drafted served two years in the army, whereas those who enlisted served a minimum of three years in whatever branch of service they chose.

Not many civilian firms wanted a nineteen-year-old with little or no skills or education. But the army took such young people and made them cooks and truck drivers, riflemen and artillerymen, supply specialists and clerks. During brief periods when the military needed many men, such as during a huge troop call-up in the fall of 1966, some men who were drafted were inducted into the marines. The army and marines believed the draftees were ready for Vietnam after they had seen six weeks of basic training and eight weeks of advanced training.

As the war ground on, the military was less particular about whom it took. In mid-1966, a U.S. Army platoon (about forty soldiers) of basic trainees at Fort Knox, Kentucky, included one man who had only one lung, a man who had been released early from the penitentiary in Jackson, Michigan, because he promised to enlist, and individuals with poor vision, missing fingers, low intelligence-test scores, or several dependents. Most either made it through six weeks of training or were recycled and took the six-week course a second time. The former inmate lasted three weeks before running away, getting caught, and being returned to Michigan to serve the remainder of his prison sentence.

A Soldier's Pay

Pay was ninety dollars a month for a new inductee, known as a private E-1. Married soldiers were paid twice that, with half of the total automatically sent to each soldier's wife. Because a woman could not live anywhere in the country on ninety dollars a month, wives frequently moved in with family and worked outside the home. If the woman was a mother, she had little choice but to move in with one set of parents or the other, even though she received some money for the child. By the time most men got to Vietnam, they were privates first-class, which earned them about two hundred dollars monthly, including combat pay, with a similar amount paid to their wives. Married men with more than one child usually were not drafted because the larger the soldier's family, the more support money the government had to pay them.

The average draftee was a single white male with a high school education from a town or small city. He lived with his parents, owned a car on which he was making payments, and was earning approximately $120 in take-home pay a week at a full-time job when ordered to report for induction. Fathers of many of these young men were World War II or Korean War veterans who felt that serving the country was an honorable thing. Most draftees did not try to avoid service, though as the war continued, more and more refused to report for duty. By 1970 in California, for example, only about two-thirds of those ordered to report showed up. Without skills or education, such a draftee was likely to become a combat infantryman.

Minorities in the Military

Minorities made up a large percentage of the military, although the air force and especially the navy had a reputation for accepting whites and rejecting everyone else at the time because of systematic discrimination

These U.S. Army soldiers are survivors of an ambush in a rubber plantation in central Vietnam in 1965. Vietcong and North Vietnamese forces usually attacked only when they outnumbered U.S. or South Vietnamese forces.

and inherent racism. Those who served in Vietnam represented a broad spectrum of ethnic cultures.

African-Americans. Early in the war, a large number of Black soldiers found themselves in the thick of the fighting. At one point, 23 percent of those killed were Black, even though only 11 percent of all American citizens were Black. When this was brought to the attention of the military and the public, matters improved to some extent; fewer Blacks were assigned frontline duties and more provided noncombat support services. Still, many young white Americans continued to stay out of the military by attending college. African-Americans also were an unwilling part of a Johnson administration fiasco called Project 100,000. This effort to draft 100,000 young Americans who might otherwise end up jobless or in jail or prison sometimes thrust minorities onto the frontlines.

If, for African-Americans, the Vietnam War had a watershed, it was the 1968 assassination of Dr. Martin Luther King, Jr. Black soldiers, angry and demoralized, turned on their military superiors. Racial incidents became increasingly common. African-Americans marched on a commanding general's quarters in Chu Lai, South Vietnam, in 1971, and there was a weeklong race riot at the big air base in Da Nang and at Camp Baxter near Vietnam's demilitarized zone. In the states, there were 160 racial incidents at the U.S. Marine base in Camp Lejeune, North Carolina, alone, and rioting took place at Travis Air Force base in California.

Ironically, the Vietnam War was the first major conflict where African-Americans were given relatively equal opportunity with whites, at least in the army. The marines had long been known for racism, and the navy was the place where Blacks were most likely to be kept in low-level positions supervised by whites. Nevertheless, figures compiled in 1973 show that 275,827 African-Americans served in the military during the Vietnam era, 41,770 served in Vietnam, and 5,570 were killed.

Hispanic-Americans. No exact figures are available, but a large number of Latinos served their country during the period 1964 to 1975. There was no ethnic group more diverse. One person with a Hispanic surname

The first prisoner of war

Responding on August 4, 1964, to the possibly phony report of U.S. Navy ships under attack, jet aircraft were launched off the aircraft carrier *Constellation*. Lieutenant (junior grade) Everett Alvarez, Jr., from San Jose, California, was among the first pilots to be catapulted from the carrier. He joined his squadron, which consisted of ten planes, as the sleek craft headed toward North Vietnam. This was Alvarez's first combat experience. It would also prove to be his last.

Two hours later, the planes made one pass to confirm that their target was an oil depot, then circled and came in low, firing rockets. Alvarez remembers that he was very low, "just skimming the trees at about five hundred knots." He felt a jolt, and his aircraft began to come apart, rolling over and burning. Realizing that he would be killed if he stayed with the damaged plane, Alvarez ejected and was hurled into space, still strapped to his cockpit seat. As his parachute opened, he cleared a cliff and landed in shallow water, suffering a broken back.

Local militia quickly arrived and took the dazed young U.S. Navy officer to a nearby jail. He was visited there by Pham Van Dong, North Vietnam's prime minister, who had been in the area when the attack occurred. Alvarez was taken later to North Vietnam's most infamous prisoner-of-war camp, the grim "Hanoi Hilton." He was the first of six hundred airmen captured by the communists, and he was held until the cease-fire agreement was signed more than eight years later.

might have been a middle-class Florida surfer whose family had lived in a part of North America that is now the United States for three hundred years. Another could have been a resident of Puerto Rico, drafted even though he did not understand one word of English. A third might have been a first-generation Mexican-American living on a small ranch in a remote part of Texas.

Besides heritage, the only thing these soldiers shared was a tradition of military service. Historically, Hispanics came out of the fields, factories, and shops to distinguish themselves for a country that paid them little attention. Many veterans recall the stereotype of the *macho* (brave male) Hispanic in action. This macho tradition sometimes put more pressure on the individual soldier than he could bear. Hispanics and other minorities sometimes identified with the Vietnamese, whom they saw as being victimized by whites.

Native Americans. A total of eighty-two thousand American Indians served in the military during the Vietnam era. That is the highest per capita number of any ethnic group. Close to 90 percent of these young men enlisted, showing a strong preference for the Marines or the Army. Consequently, their losses were heavy: three thousand of the fifty-eight thousand American dead were Native people. More than 30 percent were wounded, an indication that many Native Americans were on the front lines.

Why were Native Americans eager to fight? Veterans who survived point out their strong warrior tradition. People living on a reservation recall that the military was "a way of getting away . . . it was something to do." Reservation residents were often sent proudly off to war following tribal recognition. In combat, some platoon and squad leaders assumed Native Americans were "natural" fighters and too frequently said, "Hey Chief, you take the point." (The point is the dangerous lead position in a line of soldiers out on patrol). This may have been done innocently enough, but it cost many American Indians their lives.

Asian-Americans. Americans of Asian descent who served in Vietnam often reported being compared to the Vietnamese by their fellow soldiers. They and Native Americans tell of being approached by Vietnamese, who

A blind Vietnamese girl with a head injury is treated in 1967 by a U.S. Air Force major as part of a program to improve the health of Vietnamese civilians. Many Vietnamese suffered from noncombat injuries and various diseases.

These three American nurses wear Purple Hearts in Saigon, South Vietnam, as evidence of their injuries in a terrorist bombing on Christmas Eve, 1964. Some ten thousand American women, most of them nurses, served in Vietnam.

would rub the soldiers' arms, rub their own arms, and murmur "same-same." An American of Japanese descent who spoke no Japanese went on leave in Japan. Many Japanese, not realizing that he was American, spoke to him only in their own language. They grew impatient when he shook his head and spoke back to them in English! Such cultural clashes, while not directly related to the war, could be frustrating and confusing to GIs who wanted to be thought of simply as Americans.

Women. Women made up 2.1 percent of those who served. Because a terrorist bomb could be planted anywhere and a midnight mortar attack could hit a hospital or office, women were sometimes in as much danger as any of the males in the same vicinity. They numbered about ten thousand, with 90 percent of all military women listed as nurses. Eight military women died in the war; five of the eight lost their lives in aircraft crashes. A number of nurses suffered posttraumatic stress disorder back in the United States because they had seen too many dying people in field-hospital operating rooms.

Immigrants and Foreign Nationals. Small numbers of foreigners signed up for the military as a way to gain U.S. citizenship. These people, often Eastern Europeans or persons from Central or South America, fared well enough if they knew English. Drawn by the prospect of good earnings, substantial numbers of nonmilitary foreigners also came to Vietnam. A Korean tailor could make good money sewing patches on uniforms, and a Filipino musician might save enough to buy some land back home. Filipino rock bands played soul music to Americans of African heritage and their Vietnamese dates in side-street bars in Saigon as the fighting raged a few miles away. Nothing about this war was easily defined or understood.

An antiwar demonstration takes place during the 1968 Democratic National Convention in Chicago. The issue of whether to continue the war divided the United States as have few other issues in its history.

CHAPTER THREE

The War at Home

Not since the Civil War a century earlier had the United States seen such widespread discontent. Between 1964, when U.S. forces joined the Vietnam War, and 1973, when the last American soldier departed, the United States split into two factions: those who backed the war and those who opposed it. The conflict itself, with its terrible waste of lives, caused much bad feeling. But other circumstances contributed to the discontent, circumstances created at and by the end of World War II.

Veterans of World War II, many of whom would send sons to Vietnam, came home in 1945 and 1946, found jobs, got married, and started families. Couples had large numbers of children, creating what would be called the baby boom. The boom lasted until around 1960, and the consequence was a huge number of Americans born in the late 1940s and throughout the 1950s. Thousands would grow up to be drafted and sent to Vietnam.

Most of these young people were born into a world of material comfort and possessions; families bought new homes, paid for new cars, purchased television sets, acquired stereophonic record players, and spent more money on their children than any generation in history. The kids were safe in new suburbs, guided by crossing guards on the way to school and by distant B-36 and B-52 bombers poised to drop nuclear weapons should the Soviet Union attack. Despite Cold War threats tossed between communist and noncommunist nations, life was good — or was it?

Life certainly had its rewards for European-Americans who were part of the middle class. But for others, notably African-Americans, life was tough and showed little improvement. President Harry S. Truman integrated the armed forces prior to the Korean War, but outfits like the U.S. Marines remained racist. Some of this came from military officers' beliefs that southern white men should lead Black soldiers because southern whites knew Blacks better and were used to handling them. The military failed to consider that the twentieth century's massive migration of Black Americans from the South to the North in search of work also was an effort to escape such treatment.

African Americans observe the birthday of the Rev. Martin Luther King, Jr., in 1971 in Long Binh, South Vietnam. A foe of the war, King had killed by a sniper's bullet in Memphis, Tennessee, three years earlier. His death sparked riots in cities across the United States.

Numerous military bases were in the southern U.S. A 1950s African American soldier from Chicago, for example, crossed the Ohio River headed for duty to find segregated drinking fountains, restrooms that were off-limits, and racially segregated movie theaters. American children of African heritage knew that the Constitution said one thing and the country, North and South, did another. If Black civil rights activism had a birth-date and a hometown, it was on December 1, 1955, in Montgomery, Alabama. There, a Black woman named Rosa Parks refused to give up her seat to a white man on a public bus, as local law demanded, and was arrested. A federal judge upheld Parks's right to sit where she pleased.

The civil rights movement was on. Television played an important role, as it would in the debate over Vietnam. Middle-class whites saw violent images on the evening news of Black Americans being beaten, blasted with fire hoses, and chewed by dogs. They began to sympathize with the activists' struggle to achieve equal education, equal access to voting booths, and equal access to government and business services.

Black and white American teenagers became convinced, perhaps by television, that theirs was an age of activism — in contrast to the conservatism that supported the status quo of the 1950s — and they began to act. Because of the baby boom, there were millions of young, energy-filled activists.

As young white people joined African-Americans in the civil rights struggle, a few young Blacks became militant. They pointed to kidnappings, tough tactics by law enforcement, and racism by leaders such as Alabama Governor George Wallace as proof that the United States would never change. A few people formed militant, paramilitary organizations such as the Black Panthers in major cities, arming themselves against the white majority.

Simultaneously, some young white people realized they did not want to be like their parents and dropped out of what they called straight (average, middle-class) society. These so-called hippies grew long hair, dressed unusually, smoked marijuana and used other drugs, and moved into low-rent sections of cities all across the country. Although these were a minority, they were vocal and highly visible.

The Black Panthers and other militants

The assassination in the spring of 1968 of Dr. Martin Luther King, Jr., sent a shiver of fear down American spines. It also sent African-Americans into the streets of major cities, where they looted and burned before being corralled by U.S. Army units and the National Guard. Prior to King's death, most Americans held out hope for racial progress without violence. But after James Earl Ray's bullet killed the Baptist minister as he stood on a Memphis motel balcony, hopes dimmed.

The Black Panthers, an African-American defense group, had been founded two years earlier by Huey Newton and Bobby Seale (pictured here) in Oakland, California. They were well funded until Newton and others turned from civil rights to Black Power, advocating force when necessary to protect Black people. The group armed itself and prepared for the worst. In less than two years, twenty-eight of its members had been killed by police, while leaders such as Newton, Seale, and Eldridge Cleaver were imprisoned, charged, and exiled, respectively. The Panthers were the most visible symbols of militant African Americans, and numerous Black members of the U.S. military adopted radical African look, dress, rituals, and slogans.

Black-militant soldiers in Vietnam gave each other complex hand signals, grew large, Afro-style hairdos (despite military regulations to the contrary), wore various medallions, and decorated flak jackets and helmets with carefully worded threats. Away from the fighting, enlisted men's clubs, which might be special tents with beer or soda and jukeboxes, frequently turned into scenes of brawls, usually between Black militants and white racists. Something as simple as the song being played could set matters off, and several deaths resulted from these fights.

Back home, Panthers sometimes recruited Vietnam vets. They also fortified themselves against law enforcement, which proved dangerous. Law enforcement took the militants' defensive attitude as indicating that the Panthers had something to hide and frequently stormed a Panther residence with major personnel and firepower. Chicago police shot two members of the Black Panthers in a predawn raid in 1970 as they lay asleep in their beds. It may seem that radical antiwar groups had little effect on the war in Vietnam, yet they set the tone for the way American soldiers saw themselves and their country.

Because such young white Americans were liable to military service, they were easily convinced that the war in Vietnam was unjust. From isolated demonstrations and informational gatherings known as teach-ins on college campuses such as the University of Michigan and the University of California, the antiwar movement grew throughout the 1960s. It is ironic that the movement was filled with middle-class white people because they were less likely to go to Vietnam and the working-class youths more likely to be drafted and serve in Vietnam supported the war. Smaller numbers of Hispanics and Blacks and very few Native Americans participated in the movement. Indians had always used the military as a way to get off the reservation, to improve their self-esteem, or to save some money, and not even an unjust war changed their needs.

But Who Wanted War?

Three presidents — John F. Kennedy, Lyndon B. Johnson, and Richard M. Nixon — were involved in the Vietnam War, yet they were influenced by their predecessors. Harry Truman, president from 1945 to 1952, was under pressure to prove that he and the Democrats were as anticommunist as the Republicans. They looked the other way as Republican Senator Joe McCarthy ruined many careers, flinging accusations of communism at everyone from movie actors to members of the U.S. Army. During the Truman and Eisenhower administrations, the United States fought a war in Korea in the belief that communism should be stopped, or contained, wherever it threatened to expand.

President John F. Kennedy and his fellow Democratic advisors were liberal cold warriors. That is, they had an agenda of social programs at home and wanted to stop communism outside U.S. borders in its tracks. Eisenhower had sent aid and a few advisors to South Vietnam, so it did not bother Kennedy to step up both aid and manpower. Robert F. Kennedy, the president's younger brother and a member of

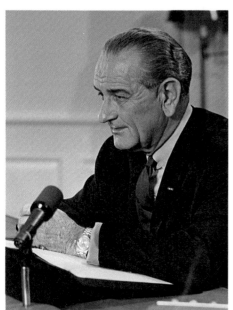

John F. Kennedy (top) greatly increased the number of U.S. military advisors in South Vietnam. His successor, Lyndon B. Johnson (above), decided against running for president in 1968 because of widespread sentiment against his Vietnam policies.

his cabinet, once suggested pulling U.S. advisors out of Vietnam. The idea fell with a thud during a meeting and was not brought up again for months. Others under the president who urged combat included Robert McNamara, secretary of defense.

Lyndon Johnson inherited many of the same advisors following the death of John Kennedy. He admired the intelligence of McNamara, who saw the growing antiwar feeling in the country and the failure of trying to bomb North Vietnam into surrender. McNamara would resign in despair in 1968.

Johnson annoyed some Americans by portraying himself as the peace candidate in the 1964 presidential election, then acting as if he was in mourning every time he announced another troop call-up for the war. The conflict also diverted attention from many of Johnson's domestic programs. The president's decision not to run for reelection in 1968 was due in part to the fact that Vietnam had pushed Democratic priorities aside, deeply dividing the party.

In contrast to Johnson, Richard M. Nixon appeared as if he paid no attention to public opinion. He actually took steps to annoy members of the antiwar movement, which continued to grow throughout his first term in office. Nixon depended on war advice from many people, but among the most frequent sources was a former Harvard professor, Henry Kissinger. Kissinger and Nixon made a number of decisions about the war that were controversial and illegal. Many were secret decisions that should have involved Congress. Nixon's willingness to violate laws would haunt him later. At one point in his first term, more than half of all Americans wanted him to immediately pull all U.S. forces out of Vietnam. Polls taken in 1967 showed that the majority of Americans believed involvement in Vietnam to be a mistake.

Richard M. Nixon promised to end U.S. involvement in Vietnam as early as 1968. Four years later, he pledged "peace with honor," which eventually meant declaring "peace" by turning over the war to the South Vietnamese. It was a phrase that rankled many Americans on both sides of the war debate.

Johnson and Nixon for years used bombing and the threat of bombing to try to persuade North Vietnam to negotiate. But the North Vietnamese steadfastly believed that the United States had no business in any part of Vietnam and therefore refused to talk. Consequently, the North endured a barrage of bombs, more than were dropped by all sides in World War II. Although oil depots and warehouses were hit, so were schools, hospitals, and homes. Civilian casualties numbered in the tens of thousands. Yet the only bombing strategy that ever had any effect on North Vietnam took place at the end of 1972, when virtually all Americans had already departed South Vietnam.

Besides public resentment and North Vietnamese steadfastness, Johnson and Nixon endured criticism from business leaders and celebrities. Lady Bird Johnson, Lyndon Johnson's wife, was cornered at many public appearances by women who told her in front of news cameras that her husband's views on the war were wrong. Richard Nixon surrounded himself with yes men, yet he saw that his only hope was Vietnamization — a gradual reduction of American forces while turning the fighting over to the South Vietnamese. The enemies list Richard Nixon's people drew up of his antiwar opponents was a virtual who's who of Hollywood, television, the recording industry, and other moguls and stars.

War News

One of the reasons so many Americans even had an opinion on the war was the thoroughness of its coverage. Americans with loved ones in Vietnam lost their appetites as they saw the wounded and the dying on both sides during the evening news. Cringing in a bunker as rockets and mortars blew

The news media helped uncover the massacre at My Lai, South Vietnam, where between one hundred and six hundred innocent civilians were slaughtered by young and inexperienced U.S. troops in late 1968.

up all around him, a nineteen-year-old soldier said more to a TV newsperson in ten seconds than all the politicians could proclaim in a year: "I'm just trying to do what my dad advised," he yelled above the din. "Keep my head down and my chin up."

There were few lighthearted photos coming out of Vietnam, and the pictures that were spread across newspaper pages were especially intense. Scenes from Dak To and Khe Sanh, where marines were pinned down for weeks at a time in 1967 and 1968, showed silent body bags lined up along a makeshift, perforated-metal runway. Whose son or brother or husband might be lying there? War had never been so well covered — or so disturbing.

News analysts separated into two camps — those for and those against the war. Persons who favored continuing or intensifying the fighting were called hawks. Those who favored less fighting or a pullout were called doves. Not many analysts changed their views; however, as the war progressed, the hawks claimed that the United States could not win because there were too many rules and constraints on the military. Many hawks advocated making all of Vietnam, including civilian areas, free-fire zones, and some even endorsed the use of nuclear weapons. Hawkish experts who favored a pullout said they felt America was fighting "with one hand tied behind its back." In reality, North Vietnam and the Vietcong were well trained and dedicated — much more so than the South Vietnamese.

Few means of communication were more effective than political cartoons. Newspapers and news magazines were influential at the time, and cartoonists took great delight in drawing caricatures of Lyndon Johnson, Richard Nixon, and others. Perhaps the most famous cartoon was based loosely on fact. President Johnson had minor surgery in 1965 and lifted his pajama top afterward to show the news media the scar. A political cartoonist drew the scene accurately, with one exception — the long, thin scar was shaped like Vietnam! By early 1971, when a poll showed that 51 percent of the population felt the war was morally wrong, few editorial writers, cartoonists, or editors supported it.

Cover-ups

In 1971, the *New York Times* published what became known as the Pentagon Papers. This huge collection of secret or confidential Department of Defense information had been photocopied by Daniel Ellsberg, a former government employee and hawk who had grown disillusioned with the war. The papers revealed a government unwilling to face the truth about Vietnam from the start. Trusted presidential advisors and other government employees were more intent on keeping secrets from the public about South Vietnamese corruption and ineptness, for example, than in truthful analysis. Despite President Nixon's efforts to halt publication of the documents, they were printed and widely read.

An earlier cover-up caused even more of a sensation. A company of U.S. Army soldiers went berserk late in 1968 in a small village in northern South Vietnam named My Lai. These infantrymen killed at least 109 and as many as 600 unarmed elderly people, women, and children after lining many of them up so that they would fall in a ditch after being shot. The shameful incident was brought to light in 1969 when a former helicopter crew member wrote to Senator Morris Udall of Arizona. Udall's investigation found the veteran's information about "dark and bloody" rumors of a massacre to be true. Several officers were punished, but not severely. The only person imprisoned was a young lieutenant named William Calley.

A group who survived the My Lai massacre. The tragedy was successfully covered up by U.S. Army officers and enlisted personnel for a year.

In 1968, Calley had found himself in charge of an infantry platoon — about thirty privates, corporals, specialists, and sergeants armed with automatic rifles, machine guns, and hand grenades. He led his men into My Lai, and many of them began to kill civilians. Although dozens of officers and enlisted personnel knew of the tragedy, they said nothing. Some kept quiet while in uniform because they feared for their lives.

A total of fourteen Army officers were charged with covering up the My Lai massacre. All of them, including Calley, entered pleas of not guilty. The lieutenant was convicted of the deaths of twenty-two civilians, his awards and decorations were taken from him, he was dishonorably discharged, and his prison sentence was reduced from life to twenty years. He was paroled after serving only four years. Hawkish Americans felt Calley took the rap for superior officers with more experience in and around My Lai. Many in the military believed Calley was the product of a system without access to people who would make good officers.

There was truth in that belief. The smartest young adults were not entering military service but were instead given deferments for college if they could afford tuition or get loans or scholarships. Those with good college grades who did not want to go to war continued to seek deferments for graduate school. Consequently, the military had to continually lower its standards to find not only officers, but enlisted personnel, as well. Calley was a Florida native who had flunked out of junior college. He had passed a test for officers' candidate school and became a second lieutenant. Calley's men included people who failed the induction intelligence test but were taken anyway. They neither knew nor cared much about the Vietnamese. College graduates did not want to be in charge of such men, so officer material remained thin.

The Antiwar Movement

Those who were against the war included most college students and millions of young people between the ages of approximately fourteen and thirty. These increasingly alienated people found the thing about adults they most disliked was hypocrisy — saying one thing and doing another. They took great pleasure in revealing the hypocrisy practiced by individuals supporting the war. For example, no son of a member of Congress was drafted into the military during the Vietnam War. If hawkish members of Congress really believed what they said, shouldn't they back it up by sending their allegedly patriotic sons to the fight?

The antiwar movement spread from college campuses to the streets. Each

The U.S. antiwar movement gained momentum steadily throughout the 1960s. Each time it lost energy, some event such as My Lai would come along, adding voices to the call for peace. This photo was taken at the 1968 Democratic Convention in Chicago during a floor demonstration against the war.

year that the war continued, the protests grew larger, and those who protested became more representative of the average American. Often, otherwise loyal members of society were almost forced by the government to condemn the war: The mother of a young Iowa farm boy who died of wounds in Vietnam resulting from U.S. weapons, or "friendly fire," made some inquiries because she wanted to know how her son's life ended. Someone in the government labeled her a troublemaker, and the Federal Bureau of Investigation shadowed this grieving parent. Small wonder that people like her questioned motives.

Others involved in the antiwar movement included huge numbers of the clergy. Religious activists such as the Reverend Martin Luther King, Jr., and Roman Catholic priests such as the Berrigan brothers opposed the war early on. They were joined by veterans of the civil rights struggle, pacifists, celebrities, hippies, and even a number of Vietnam veterans. In fact, a group that called itself Vietnam Veterans Against the War attracted much more attention than its total number, which was only about seven thousand nationwide. Members donned their uniforms to march on Washington and elsewhere in the late 1960s and early 1970s, which fascinated the news media.

What did these veterans against the war know that civilians did not? They had seen the corruption so prevalent in Vietnam, where U.S. soldiers

Members of Vietnam Veterans Against the War march toward the site of the Democratic National Convention in Miami in 1972. Though small in number, antiwar vets made people think about the situation in Vietnam.

could not buy their favorite brand of beer, soda, or cigarettes on their military bases but could buy stolen beer, soda, or cigarettes on the Saigon black market. The veterans knew that few officers or enlisted people wanted to be in Vietnam and that the military often sent soldiers into dangerous areas to draw fire without any real plan. Vets knew how hard it was to tell friend from foe in the jungles or rice paddies, and they realized that heat, malaria, venereal disease, and drug and alcohol abuse could disable a soldier as readily as a booby trap might. Such knowledge became widespread.

The Nixon administration, led by Secretary of Defense Melvin Laird, decided to pacify U.S. war foes with a new plan. The watchword following Nixon's election in 1968 became *Vietnamization* — meaning the United States would gradually withdraw troops, turning more and more of the fighting over to the South Vietnamese. Laird and others believed that troop reductions would please antiwar foes, whose numbers now included half of Congress. U.S. troop strength declined from 540,000 at the end of 1968 to 480,000 at the end of 1969. Although the theory behind Vietnamization was sound, it had one undesirable effect: new soldiers who arrived in Vietnam did so with an attitude.

No one wanted to be the last man to die for a losing cause. Peace signs were drawn on flak jackets, and marijuana use became almost epidemic. Soldiers on patrol refused orders they thought were wrong or dangerous, and inflexible officers were often "fragged" — blown up with hand grenades — by their own men. Though they hung together under fire in the field, soldiers divided into hippies, Blacks, and southerners in base camps, sometimes with violent results. Camp LBJ (the Long Binh Jail) housed drug- and alcohol-crazed soldiers whom even the well-armed camp guards found frightening.

Other Opponents of the War

As if the United States did not have enough problems, many allies became distant. Canada allowed U.S. citizens to remain in that country if they were there to avoid the draft. French president Charles de Gaulle chided the United States constantly. West Germans not only disapproved of U.S. involvement in Southeast Asia but also complained about the number of U.S. bases on German soil. Worse, German radicals harassed U.S. business and military people. Great Britain was virtually the only consistent friend throughout the war, although other countries sent troops to Vietnam.

Those countries included Australia, Korea, New Zealand, the Philippines, and Thailand. The Thais were ruled by a military dictatorship that welcomed U.S. air bases. From these sites, aircraft attacked North Vietnam and enemy targets in Laos and South Vietnam for years.

The Vietnamese reacted calmly to the mix of people in uniform — older residents of the country could recall a rich stew of nationalities in the French Foreign Legion that tried unsuccessfully to oust communism after World War II. In contrast, American GIs thought all Vietnamese looked alike, though many actually were ethnically Cambodians, Chinese, or rural people the French called Montagnards.

These citizens from other countries posed a problem for U.S. military strategists. The Soviets and the Chinese ran freighters filled with weapons and supplies in and out of Haiphong, North Vietnam's port. The com-

An Australian soldier bargains with a Vietnamese man over a Christmas tree at an outdoor market in Saigon in 1966. Troops from several nations came to the aid of the South Vietnamese.

munist nations threatened action if U.S. planes dropped bombs on their ships. Equally important, U.S. airmen had to be careful as they neared the North Vietnam border with China. War goods streamed into Vietnam there, but pilots faced a dogfight if they strayed over Chinese territory. The North Vietnamese had a few Soviet MIG fighter planes, but they were no match for the variety of supersonic aircraft thrown at them. Luckily for U.S. pilots, the Chinese and the North Vietnamese had a falling out, and the stream of Chinese materials decreased.

War in the Air and on the Ground

What made the military situation more even — and resulted in hundreds of U.S. pilots being downed — was the antiaircraft fire that greeted every U.S. mission. In addition to guns of various sizes, the North Vietnamese used missiles that locked on a plane and were fired, catching up with the craft, often with fatal results. These radar-guided missiles sent out a signal that U.S. jets could pick up. The jets fired rockets back down the radar signal, sometimes hitting the missile site. American pilots knew to take evasive

action due to a device that sounded an alarm whenever enemy radar locked on their planes. This form of warfare was expensive, highly technical, and nerve shattering.

Equally worrisome was ground combat, which continued into the 1970s. Day after day, year after year, Americans and their allies searched rice paddies, jungles, mountains, and villages for the enemy. Communist soldiers seldom stuck around for a pitched battle — unless they greatly outnumbered U.S. forces. Whenever a firefight occurred, Americans called in artillery, air strikes, and helicopter gunships. If the Vietcong or the North Vietnamese seemed to be losing the battle, they would slip silently away, usually taking their dead and sometimes hiding in tunnels with secret entrances. GIs worried when the enemy got the upper hand: It was understood that Americans who were overrun were usually executed.

Helicopters bring supplies to embattled Khe Sanh, an outpost defended by U.S. Marines in 1968. Americans feared that the remote fire base would become another Dien Bien Phu, where French forces surrendered in 1954.

Only one U.S. soldier in eight was designated a frontline fighter, but everyone from the cooks to the clerk-typists to the supply sergeants pulled guard duty. This involved sitting in a foxhole all night long around the perimeter of a base, making sure that no enemy came near. Soldiers performing guard duty were armed with M-16 automatic rifles and might have a hand-held trigger attached to a claymore mine. These mines, which resembled Polaroid cameras, were placed in front of the foxhole on short tripods. They were designed to stop large numbers of charging enemy soldiers by blowing jagged metal across a wide area.

The Tet Offensive

War in the air, war in the jungle, war all night long, war in its many forms contributed to the uneasy mood at home. Nothing, however, shook the United States like the battles that took place in Vietnam's major cities early in 1968. The North Vietnamese and the Vietcong traditionally had operated in remote areas. But during the Vietnamese New Year, known as Tet, communist soldiers invaded cities and attacked military bases all across the

country. And although their losses were staggering, it was a psychological victory for the communists. The carefully coordinated attack played a large part in turning even more Americans against the war.

Tet began with festive fireworks on the night of January 30, 1968, and ended with gunfire as guerrillas stormed Saigon, Hue, Da Nang, and other cities, killing American and South Vietnamese soldiers and civilians. Noncommunist forces reacted well, although Vietcong guerrillas got inside the U.S. embassy compound and had to be hunted down and killed one by one. Fighting in Saigon was vicious as retreating enemy soldiers set fires and killed the innocent. But it ended in three days. In contrast, U.S. Marines and Army of the Republic of Vietnam (ARVN) troops battled as a team to gain control of the city of Hue in house-to-house fighting for three weeks. Tet caused Walter Cronkite, the most respected person in television news, to blurt, "I thought we were winning the war!"

The war, to most U.S. civilians, simply did not seem winnable. Television showed Marines in far outposts like Dak To or Khe Sanh, not fighting but hanging on as they were shelled night and day. Others saw U.S. Army troops slogging through rice-paddy mud that looked like oatmeal in the Mekong Delta. Many troops died without ever seeing the enemy. What kind of war was this, Americans wondered. No one had an honest, ready answer.

U.S. Marines fill sandbags for protection during a lull in the shelling at Khe Sanh. Enemy soldiers, hidden in the hills in the background, pounded the fire base for several weeks before withdrawing.

America's first armed forces draft lottery since the dawn of World War II takes place on December 1, 1969. The blue capsules hold slips of paper indicating birthdates of potential draftees.

CHAPTER FOUR

The War Winds Down

One evening in 1969, three college sophomores gathered around the television set in their apartment. They awaited news of a government program that would affect their lives. Shortly after 8:00 P.M., numbers from 1 through 365 began to be matched with randomly drawn dates. Among the first drawn was October 24, the birthday of one of the trio. Near tears, the nineteen-year-old called his parents. Another saw that his date of birth matched the 240th number. He wondered: Would he be called? The final youth became happier as more and more dates were picked. By the time his date of birth matched the 339th number, he was jubilant. What was going on?

Even college students, who had received deferments, considered the draft unfair. Why should some young men be exempt? In an effort to make the military draft equitable, the Selective Service System went to a lottery-type call-up. No longer would students be granted automatic deferments so they could stay in college year after year. Now, if their date of birth matched a low number, they would be drafted. It was widely reported that the first 200 dates would be called up and that persons with dates matching numbers from about 250 to 365 had little to worry about.

Protests at Home Help End the War

By the end of 1969, U.S. troop strength in Vietnam had grown to 480,000. And so, although the lottery allayed the fears of many American families even as it stoked the fears of others, it did not alter opposition to the war itself. Young people tangled with police in a riot at the 1968 Democratic National Convention in Chicago. The nationally televised battle indicated youthful disapproval of the Democratic Party's refusal to turn against the war and police impatience with demonstrators. Priests, nuns, and others earnestly trying to bring the war to the nation's attention were clubbed to the ground. Not even the headquarters of Eugene McCarthy, an antiwar Democratic presidential candidate, were off-limits to the police.

A smaller but attention-getting protest took place at Kent State University in Ohio in 1970. National Guardsmen, harassed by college students,

An antiwar demonstrator wounded by armed National Guard troops is placed into an ambulance at Kent State University, Ohio, on May 4, 1970. Four students died in the tragedy, which caused unrest at campuses all across the country.

shot four of them to death and wounded others as the students protested the illegal U.S. invasion of Cambodia. Americans attributed the actual invasion to the scheming of President Richard M. Nixon and his national security advisor, Henry Kissinger.

Dozens of colleges were soon shut down by antiwar activists. One remarkable thing about events such as Kent State is that every time the antiwar movement appeared to lose energy, news events reenergized it. These events could happen on the other side of the globe, or they could take place on a usually peaceful college campus in the Midwest. The end result was continued suspicion and dislike of the American government and of those who ran it.

African-Americans let their feelings be known, too. Every summer from 1965 to the late 1960s, the sultry air of cities all over the country was filled with the smell of smoke, the flash of broken glass, and the wail of sirens. Rioting Black Americans were incensed about the war, but the war was only one of many things that angered them. Persons of African heritage felt as strongly as any time in history that justice did not work for them — in the courts, in the streets, on the job, or in a combat zone. Such thoughts were the same ones that ignited the civil rights movement, but these riots were a violent contrast to what had been peaceful protests early in the 1960s. Small wonder that there were riots in inner cities — 90 percent of those on welfare and 92 percent of jail inmates were nonwhite, according to figures put together in 1968.

In contrast, most members of the New Left were neither poor nor members of minority groups. Rather, they were usually sons and daughters of middle-class professionals. Many dabbled in antiwar activity while young, rural, southern white men and women became more conservative and backed the war. Vietnam veterans, whether white or members of ethnic

A burglary helps halt the bombing

Richard Nixon's biggest battle besides the Vietnam War — one that he would lose — quickly grabbed public attention in 1973. A group of burglars had been caught in George McGovern's Washington, D.C., campaign headquarters in 1972, and investigators found that the orders for the break-in at the Watergate Hotel came from the White House. During Senate hearings, John Dean, an attorney who served as Nixon's special counsel, publicly accused the president of breaking the law. Others pointed out that the paranoid president had taped conversations that might have included planning the Watergate break-in.

Richard Nixon had boasted of "peace with honor" in Vietnam as his presidency began to decompose. He resigned to avoid impeachment in 1974.

Watergate affected Vietnam in at least one important way. In 1973, Congress passed a bill — and overrode President Nixon's veto of that bill — to limit the president's power to begin or continue a conflict. Congressional members strengthened their influence in future warmaking decisions at a time when the current president could do little about such a move.

Prince Norodom Sihanouk cleverly kept Cambodia neutral for a number of years. He was overthrown by pro-U.S. military officers, who were opposed by communist guerrillas calling themselves Khmer Rouge, or Red Cambodians.

groups, came home and chose sides while they tried to rid themselves of the physical, mental, and emotional burden of the war.

Pursuing the Enemy

Meanwhile, in Southeast Asia, the war seemed to become more brutal as it wound down. Cambodia, under the leadership of Prince Norodom Sihanouk, had skillfully kept itself neutral since World War II. But this peaceful situation started to unravel for Vietnam's neighbor to the west when U.S. planes secretly bombed communists hiding in Cambodia in 1969. The U.S. military knew that Vietnamese communists were using Cambodia as a base of operations and that Prince Sihanouk had neither the military power nor the motivation to throw them out of his country. Consequently, U.S. bombs rained on rural Cambodia in a broad area west of Saigon. The bombing was unsuccessful as most communists in the area hid or fled temporarily westward, away from Vietnam. As rural peasants cringed during the bombing

Khmer Rouge soldiers were ragged but determined. Under their leader, Pol Pot, they killed millions of their fellow Cambodians after taking over the country in 1975.

raids, numerous sons and daughters of the country's small middle class joined the *Khmer Rouge* (Red Cambodians), guerrilla fighters who lived in remote areas and harassed Sihanouk forces. The bombing increased the number of people who took up arms against Sihanouk, and people within the Cambodian military decided to act before things got out of control.

Cambodian generals waited until the still-popular prince was out of the country. Then, the pro-U.S. military took over the government, in part because they disliked Sihanouk's policy of neutrality for their country. Pro-U.S. and communist Cambodians clashed viciously in the field; frequently, innocent civilians were gunned down just for target practice. The Khmer Rouge, mostly armed by the North Vietnamese, often got the upper hand. Shortly before American bombing ended in 1973, a misguided bomb hit a Cambodian city, killing 125 civilians. Such a tragedy came as both a political and a military blow to Lon Nol, the man who had overthrown Sihanouk and who had suffered a stroke when he learned that North Vietnamese units had attacked some of his forces. By 1975, the Khmer Rouge, led by Pol Pot, had taken over the country.

In Laos, things were almost as grim. Thinly populated and marked by mountainous jungle, Laos was the scene of a civil war, with the U.S. Central Intelligence Agency and the North Vietnamese on opposite sides. This little war never made headlines until U.S. and South Vietnamese forces entered Laos in 1971 in order to block the Ho Chi Minh trail. The noncommunist troops managed to cut the trail briefly and cause confusion, but the North Vietnamese were quickly reinforced and attacked with a vengeance. U.S. helicopter pilots probably saw the heaviest fire of the entire war as they covered troops returning to South Vietnam.

POWs and MIAs in Southeast Asia

The United States kept close track of the number of American service personnel who had been taken prisoner by the North Vietnamese. The vast majority of prisoners in North Vietnam and Laos were air crewmen. Unless a fellow flyer saw a craft explode in midair or crash without absolutely any sign of life, pilots and crew were considered missing in action (MIA) rather than dead. During almost ten years of fighting, as many as 2,477 men were reported missing. Of that number, half are known to have been killed in action. At present, about 500 are regarded as genuine

This Khmer Rouge woman is armed with an American-made M-16 semiautomatic rifle. The weapon probably was lost or left behind by U.S. forces departing Vietnam.

MIAs. About 600 prisoners of war (POWs), most of them pilots, were returned to U.S. officials when the war ended.

Most POWs suffered physical and emotional hardship in enemy hands. They were deprived of knowledge of their families, of fellow prisoners, and of current events. The flyers were usually gaunt from lack of food, and they endured long and intense interrogations. Their prison, often the old and bleak "Hanoi Hilton," was cold and wet in the winter and stifling in the summer. Some prisoners had wounds that were infected, and others lived with broken bones that were not always properly set. To make matters worse, not even the Red Cross was allowed to maintain contact with them.

The lives of captive airmen were terrible, but frontline army and marine troops faced a much worse fate — almost certain death — if they fell into enemy hands. Those who carried handguns, such as crew members of armored personnel carriers or tanks, joked that they always saved one bullet in case they were overrun by Vietcong or North Vienamese Army (NVA) soldiers. Suicide was preferable to death at the hands of the enemy, a death that could be prolonged and gruesome. Although hundreds of captured airmen eventually found their way home, very few army or marine enlisted personnel termed missing ever were heard from again.

A number of men who were known to be dead were listed as missing so their families would continue to receive pay and benefits until the soldier

A U.S. Marine Corps veteran in a Washington, D.C., ceremony honors American prisoners of war he and others believe to be held in Southeast Asia. The combat boots represent the missing.

Journalist Sean Flynn was one of several people covering the war who were either killed or reported missing in action. Flynn and a friend were marched off by an armed guerrilla and never seen again.

was officially declared dead. Occasionally, film shot by East Germans and other pro-North Vietnamese people would be shown on American television. Relatives saw, or convinced themselves they saw, missing members of their families. At other times, the North Vietnamese would parade thin, silent captives in front of television cameras. The strain of such events was terribly hard on mothers and fathers, brothers and sisters, wives and children.

The war was an equal-opportunity destroyer. When a mortar or rocket or artillery shell went off, it cut a swath through a unit without regard to race, age, or whether the victims were rookies or "short timers" — soldiers whose yearlong tour of duty was scheduled to end soon. Those who covered the war also died. Bernard Fall, a French scholar and journalist who wrote *Street Without Joy* and had been in Vietnam on and off since French occupation, was killed in 1967 when he stepped on a mine while accompanying U.S. troops. Journalist Sean Flynn was captured near the Cambodian border and never seen again. And veteran *Life* magazine photographer Larry Burrows was killed while covering the invasion of Laos.

There were several differences between this war and any war previously fought by U.S. troops. A soldier in Vietnam felt little allegiance to his unit. The only thing that mattered was the number of days he had left to serve before being shipped back to the United States. The one-year tour was a source of hope, but it also caused instability for those who neared their departure date and feared being killed at the last minute. Despite the fact that the military was better fed and better equipped than ever, the degree of complaining and dislike for the war was much higher in Vietnam than in other conflicts.

Drug Use

Partly to numb the terror of possible death, one American in four in uniform in Vietnam tried some form of illegal drug. When the officers and career soldiers are factored out of the percentage, almost half of all U.S. troops remain. With pocket change, these troops could easily buy enough powerful marijuana to stay

Life photographer Larry Burrows died in 1971 when his helicopter was shot down.

Women who served, women who died

Approximately ten thousand women, soldiers and civilians, served or worked in Vietnam from the time of the Tonkin Gulf incident to the fall of Saigon. Nine of every ten military women were nurses. Eight military women who died are remembered on the black granite wall of the Vietnam Veterans Memorial, along with the thousands of servicemen who died or were killed. Five of the eight died when their aircraft crashed or was shot from the sky. One woman died in a rocket attack, and two others died of natural causes.

There is a special memorial to women who served in the war near the main Vietnam memorial in Washington, D.C. The Vietnam Women's Memorial Project spearheaded a fund drive that finally resulted in recognition for female contributions.

Next to the military, the biggest contingent of women sent to Vietnam may have been Red Cross workers. These young Americans were requested by the military for morale reasons. They helped GIs with things like emergency messages home and straightening out support payments for wives and children. Three of these women also died — one in a Jeep accident, one from disease, and one was murdered in her sleep.

Vietcong and North Vietnamese forces also depended on women in noncombat roles. Numerous women served as nurses, working under terrible conditions underground as B-52 bombers pounded the area with a carpet of bombs. Vietcong women often were wives and mothers by day and nurses, cooks, or builders of booby traps by night. There are no accurate records concerning the deaths of Vietcong or North Vietnamese women, nor is it always possible to tell civilians from guerrilla or military personnel.

Bangkok, Thailand, with its exotic nightlife, was one of several sites where American GIs could spend a week of leave during their tour of duty in Vietnam.

high all day. Often, the marijuana was soaked in opium, which made it even more potent. U.S. troops sometimes purchased packages of filter cigarettes and gave them to local Vietnamese. The Vietnamese sold the packages back to the troops with tobacco replaced by marijuana!

Heroin was as commonly sold in parts of the country as chewing gum in the United States. The drug was snorted or injected, addicting many servicemen. Surveys showed that a large number of heroin users were Black, possibly because African-Americans had a more fatalistic attitude about the military and so feared heroin less. Some medics, who carried morphine into the field for use on wounded soldiers, were a source of small injecting needles called Syrettes.

Heroin was smuggled from the Golden Triangle, a site where the countries of Burma, Laos, and Thailand meet, into Vietnam and then on to the United States. Some of the smuggling was done by individuals, but much of it was well organized and involved military planes and officers on very different missions. From the United States came a steady supply of amphetamines ("speed") and the hallucinogen LSD. Tensions between officers and soldiers could reach the breaking point over drug use.

GIs who returned to the United States hooked on heroin were given drug-treatment opportunities as the war wound down. Not all of them submitted to drug rehabilitation. More typically, a returning soldier might begin to hang out with civilians who were frequent users or sellers of illegal drugs.

Drugs were used in base camps but seldom in the field. Soldiers usually moved through the bush during daylight hours, but they feared becoming a target by lighting any kind of smoking device once it grew dark. But base camps and long nights on guard duty resulted in many soldiers becoming high on one substance or another. One survey, conducted in 1970, estimated that sixty-five thousand U.S. soldiers were on drugs in Vietnam.

Drugs and sex made Bangkok, Thailand, one of the most popular spots for R and R (rest and recreation) — the one week of leave every soldier earned while serving in Vietnam. Numerous soldiers returned from Thailand having smoked Thai stick, an especially strong form of marijuana. Many also contracted a venereal disease, usually a form of gonorrhea that could be cured with penicillin. Marijuana and prostitutes were available in many other R and R destinations, including Hawaii, Hong Kong, the Philippines, and Taiwan.

The Failure of Vietnamization

Vietnamization should have worked. There were millions of South Vietnamese, and with modern U.S. weapons, they were better equipped than the enemy to fight the war. But the Army of the Republic of Vietnam was rotten from the top down. Soldiers were not always paid because their commanders had spent the money, wealthy Vietnamese could buy their way out of military service, and many ARVN members believed they would be saved by the United States whenever they got into serious trouble. Equally inept were local militias. These were made up of farmers and others who worked by day and guarded their villages by night. Some were Vietcong, and others

North Vietnam's Le Duc Tho (waving, left) and Henry Kissinger greet the press after meeting on January 23, 1973, in Paris to finalize the peace agreement that ended U.S. participation in the war in Vietnam.

were easy targets for the enemy. Many weapons given to local militias ended up in enemy hands.

Meanwhile, the United States did several less-than-honorable things in propping up South Vietnam. One was to look the other way when non-communist dissidents were tortured or imprisoned. Another, conceived by the Central Intelligence Agency, was Operation Phoenix. Phoenix began in 1967 and was considered at the time a U.S. solution to a Vietnamese problem. Phoenix involved South Vietnamese government officials gathering information about communists among the peasant population, then arresting or killing these communists. By 1969, some 19,534 Vietcong organizers had been killed — without trial or any other form of justice. Some may well have been ordinary people whom the government simply hated.

When Americans learned of programs such as Phoenix, they turned increasingly against the war. Secret moves by Henry Kissinger, who seemed to be engaged for years in talks with the North Vietnamese in Paris, also added to the antiwar ranks. As U.S. soldiers of all ages, races, and creeds continued to die in Southeast Asia, Kissinger and Le Duc Tho, a senior member of the North Vietnamese government, met from 1970 to early 1973, arguing over concessions. Ho Chi Minh had died of natural causes in 1969, but that seemed to make the enemy all the more determined to reunite Vietnam.

South Vietnamese President Nguyen Van Thieu was forced to fight communism without the aid of U.S. forces after the spring of 1973. U.S. aid to the South Vietnamese also dwindled between 1973 and 1975, when communist forces overran Saigon.

Scandals and Surprise Offensives

In South Vietnam, scandals continued to surface. A group of special forces led by Colonel Robert Rheault was charged with the execution of a Vietcong spy. Another group of Green Berets was caught dabbing chicken blood on Vietcong flags and selling them as souvenirs of the war! Many returning Vietnam veterans told tales of atrocities, which were not always true. Such conduct made continuing the war even more difficult for President Nixon; the size and number of antiwar rallies grew during his years in office.

Richard Nixon and everyone else realized that the quality of leadership in South Vietnam was terri-

The ordeal of Muhammad Ali

Cassius Clay was a brash, talented young boxer from Louisville, Kentucky. An Olympic gold-medal winner in 1960, he gained strength and speed and became a professional fighter. Four years later, he knocked out Sonny Liston to win the world's heavyweight championship.

Clay became a Muslim and changed his name to Muhammad Ali. He told reporters that he was a devout follower of Islam. The boxer received his draft notice in 1967 and initially flunked the intelligence test given all potential soldiers. "I said I was the greatest, not the smartest," Ali quipped. But he passed a subsequent test and refused to enter the military when ordered to report.

The World Boxing Association did not believe that Ali was the pacifist he claimed to be. Because of Ali's supposed lack of patriotism, they awarded the heavyweight title to another fighter, Joe Frazier. Ali appealed his draft notice on the grounds that his religion did not permit him to kill a fellow human. It was not until 1974 that he was exonerated and could reclaim the boxing crown, which he did.

Ali was a constant source of outrage and amusement, his handsome face gracing magazine covers and his clever remarks making for good copy. He alienated hawkish Americans who believed no one could be a pacifist and pound an opponent senseless with his fists. On the other hand, Ali made many people of all colors who paid attention only to sports take notice about the war. He also stuck to his principles regarding the lack of social justice in his own country when he declared, "No Vietcong ever called me a nigger."

ble. Nguyen Van Thieu had been president since 1967. Reelected as the only person running in 1972, Thieu was indecisive and was scorned by everyone but the inept people he picked to lead the military and the government. The war might well have ended sooner if Nixon and Kissinger had bowed to the North Vietnamese demand that Thieu be removed. Although ARVN forces outnumbered the Vietcong and the North Vietnamese Army five to one in South Vietnam, the inferior leadership handpicked by President Thieu almost always assured victory on the battlefield for communist forces.

The communists launched a dry-season offensive almost every year, and, amazingly, every year the series of attacks caught the South Vietnamese by surprise. In 1972, the same thing happened — North Vietnamese captured the major South Vietnamese city of Quangtri.

This time, President Nixon reacted by ordering bombing of military targets around Hanoi and Haiphong. One month later, Nixon went a step farther and ordered the mining of the harbor at Haiphong, despite the fact that Soviet and other ships docked there. The air war had been going on in the skies over Vienam with numerous pauses for seven years, but it was never more intense than in 1972.

Bach Mai

Doctors and nurses carry medical supplies out of the destroyed Bac Mai Hospital in Hanoi. The hospital was accidentally hit by U.S. bombers during an air raid on December 19, 1972. Despite precautions, many North Vietnamese civilians died during the years of bombing.

A Glimmer of Hope

Between the bombing and the ongoing negotiations between Henry Kissinger and the North Vietnamese in Paris, there appeared to be hope for a cease-fire. But President Thieu opposed every agreement presented to him by the United States.

To pressure President Thieu, Hanoi radio broadcast details of the peace proposals, intending to prove to the South Vietnamese people that peace was at hand but that Thieu was standing in the way. As Richard Nixon was winning reelection in a landslide over Democratic peace candidate George McGovern, Henry Kissinger was presenting dozens of amendments to a peace agreement. Le Duc Tho agreed to talk about peace, but the talks ground to a halt in December. Would this war never end?

On December 18, 1972, Nixon ordered the heaviest bombing ever of the North. Huge B-52 bombers and other U.S. planes dropped forty thousand tons of bombs on Hanoi, Haiphong, and the area between the two cities. The raids were condemned by everyone from Pope Paul VI to the French, but tales of "carpet bombing" (a series of bombs devastating a large area uniformly) were somewhat exaggerated. Although the bombs hit a hospital and killed many civilians, the bombings were planned to avoid casualties among the nonmilitary population. The U.S. lost twenty-six planes and the North Vietnamese fired fifteen hundred surface-to-air missiles before North Vietnam agreed on December 30 to return to the bargaining table.

The talks resumed in January 1973, and an agreement quickly followed. Thieu was given an ultimatum — either agree to the peace that had been negotiated or lose the support of the United States. The leader of South Vietnam had no choice but to go along with the program. Thieu would continue to receive aid from the United States, but U.S. ground forces were already all but gone by the time the agreement was hammered out. The threat that U.S. aircraft and troops could return was blunted that summer, as both the U.S. Senate and the House of Representatives voted against raising money to make war anywhere in Indochina. For America, the war was over. Vietnam was quickly forgotten — except by those who served and suffered.

A U.S. Air Force B-52 aircraft drops 750-pound bombs on Viet Cong targets in South Vietnam. B-52 crews flew out of Thailand and from U.S. bases in the western Pacific Ocean.

A disabled Vietnam veteran wipes away a tear during ceremonies at the Vietnam Memorial in 1986. The flag behind the tablets is made of fifty-eight thousand flowers and represents the Americans who died in Vietnam.

CHAPTER FIVE

War's End

The last U.S. soldier left Vietnam on March 29, 1973. There remained eighty-five hundred civilians, embassy guards, and a small number of soldiers in a defense office. Since peace had been negotiated, the Vietnamese on both sides looked around to see what would happen. The United States had spent $150 billion in Vietnam, yet the South was filled with Vietcong and North Vietnamese. Prisoners of war were exchanged, and some northerners went home. The U.S. Navy in July removed mines it had laid around Haiphong, and the U.S. Congress forced President Nixon to stop the bombing of Cambodia one month later.

With U.S. air power absent, the North Vietnamese could move fresh troops and supplies down the Ho Chi Minh trail in a matter of weeks rather than months. The spring and summer of 1973 saw an estimated seventy thousand new soldiers slip quietly into the South. For the first time, numerous Soviet-made tanks and large artillery pieces moved with them. As the dry season began in November, the Vietcong overran two Army of the Republic of Vietnam (ARVN) outposts near the Cambodian border. In 1974, South Vietnamese positions in the Mekong Delta were attacked, and the North Vietnamese pounded the former U.S. air base in Da Nang with heavy shells, along with raids on several cities.

South Vietnam in Turmoil

President Thieu faced a number of problems. Despite its population, Vietnam has always been a country with a strong rural influence. The heart of Vietnam is the small farming village that dots the map from north to south. But years of fighting had driven frightened farmers away from their rice paddies and into South Vietnam's big cities. These people had nowhere to live and no way to make a living. They feared returning to their land, having seen vicious fighting there earlier and fearing booby traps and other wartime weapons. U.S. nonmilitary aid was declining, so these homeless, jobless people weren't likely to receive anything from the corrupt South Vietnamese government.

The final offensive in the Vietnam War began with the dry season in the winter of 1974-75. The North Vietnamese Army (NVA) captured Phuoc Binh, a provincial capital only sixty miles from Saigon, at Christmas, and they captured the central highlands cities of Pleiku and Kontum early in 1975. ARVN members and civilians struggled eastward to the coast as they were shelled mercilessly by the onrushing NVA. President Thieu pulled all troops out of the highlands in an effort to save southern South Vietnam. Americans still in Vietnam did what they could, but most of their work involved nonmilitary aid and efforts to find U.S. homes for Vietnamese orphans.

Army Sergeant Donald J. Rander of Baltimore greets his wife, Andreas Hair, for the first time in more than five years. Rander was a prisoner of war held captive in Vietnam from 1968 to 1973.

Those who were able and knew what was ahead left the country. Others waited apprehensively for the North Vietnamese. Cambodia fell to Khmer Rouge communists on April 17, 1975, and a surrounded Saigon was taken by the North Vietnamese and Vietcong on April 30. Laos was taken over by communists in December. One of the many classic wire-service photos from the end of the conflict shows a U.S. helicopter sitting atop the U.S. embassy as a line of fleeing people climb toward it. Except for a few diehard journalists, there were no Americans left in Vietnam by the first of May — or were there? Many prisoners of war and missing soldiers remained unaccounted for.

Meanwhile, in Cambodia after 1975, Khmer Rouge guerrillas under leader Pol Pot were killing more than one million of their fellow citizens. Pol Pot decided Cambodia, which he called Kampuchea, should rid itself of foreign influence. He ordered the deaths of anyone who might have middle-class ties, forcing residents of the capital of Phnom Penh and other cities to leave for brutal work in new agricultural areas. Simultaneously, the Khmer Rouge raided western areas of Vietnam. The Vietnamese, who had seen their relationship with China fall apart, now felt the threat of the seemingly crazed Cambodians. Without warning, the Vietnamese swept into Cambodia in 1979, installing a puppet government and chasing Pol Pot and his followers into rural, western Cambodia.

The Chinese, who had forged a relationship with Cambodia, invaded northern Vietnam early in 1979. Terrible fighting took place while the Chinese spent three weeks on the Vietnamese side of the border. This punitive campaign left the Vietnamese with little aid and few friends. Fighting broke out again in 1984 along the China-Vietnam border, an indication that the North Vietnamese were good at war but bad at peace. The United States refused for years to deal with Vietnam until a better accounting of American war prisoners and persons missing in action was provided.

Vietnam's Impact on Veterans

For returning veterans, the silence was thunderous. American veterans of previous wars had come home to ticker tape parades, loving families, welcoming friends and neighbors, employers eager to hire them whenever possible, and a city, town, or county that was proud of their service. But this war was different. There were no parties; families, friends, and neighbors were of different minds about the war; employers feared that vets were potentially violent or drug dependent; and there was little talk of adding the names of those who served to local scrolls or memorials.

Three California veterans protest the use of Agent Orange during a 1981 hunger strike near the White House in Washington, D.C. The defoliant was used widely in Vietnam and was sprayed from U.S. aircraft to deny the enemy concealment.

Not all battle scars were visible. U.S. and Vietnamese soldiers and civilians suffered from posttraumatic stress disorder, known as shell shock during World War I and combat fatigue in World War II. Posttraumatic stress disorder is a complex label for a simple yet terrible affliction — people unexpectedly relived horrors witnessed during the war. Such scenes to this day haunt the untreated, causing them to confuse past memory with current reality. Their sleep is affected; nightmares force them awake, or mental pictures of dead friends and loved ones prevent rest. Symptoms also include flashbacks, anxious moods, depression, and poor memory. As many as 30 percent of American veterans who were in combat are hit with some form of flashback or related stress problem, sometimes making each day an ordeal. Vietnamese soldiers and civilians very likely endure similar agonies.

Males didn't have all of the problems. A female nurse in Boston saw another nurse pull a pair of scissors out of her pocket. Without knowing why, the first nurse assaulted her friend. Under psychiatric care, the nurse admitted that she had once tried to aid a wounded North Vietnamese soldier. The enemy prisoner had attempted to stab her with scissors. She told two U.S. soldiers, and they hauled the Vietnamese away, apparently killing him. The nurse struggled with such memories, sleeping only when her bedroom lights were on. She relived split-second decisions as to whom she treated and whom she neglected, based on the severity of the soldiers' terrible wounds.

Some 85 percent of all women serving in Vietnam were nurses, so they were exposed to the gore caused by modern-day weaponry. The nineteen

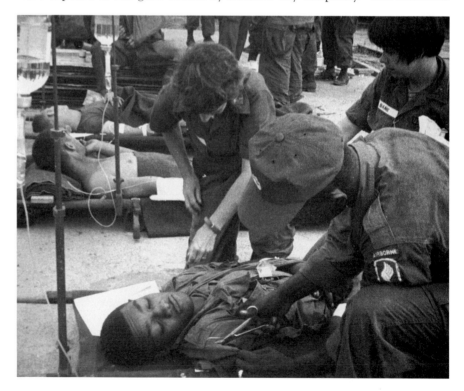

Doctors and nurses treat soldiers in the wake of a battle some thirty miles from Saigon in 1965. Sometimes overwhelmed by injured men clinging to life, doctors and nurses would later suffer vivid flashbacks and other emotional problems.

U.S. field hospitals within Vietnam saved many lives, including those of people so badly wounded that they could never again function in society. Also weighing heavily on the women were the leers, verbal abuse, and sexual harassment that followed them.

Native American veterans contrast the respect they earned in the military to the second-class treatment they received on the streets. Returnees were subjected to racist remarks, and they continued to wonder at how little most Americans knew about their history or their lives. "White people were ignorant of reservation life," a Chippewa noted. "They thought a reservation had a fence around it, that you had to get a pass to leave.

A group of marines returning from duty in Vietnam flash the peace sign and display a handmade peace symbol on the side of their amphibious warship. Although many soldiers formed their own opinions against the war while serving, they were shocked at the hostile reception that some Americans gave them back home.

And they couldn't figure out why we were so patriotic." A large number of today's Native activists are Vietnam veterans, perhaps because they learned to be leaders in the military.

For a number of Black vets, Martin Luther King, Jr., summed up the contradiction they carried: "We are taking young black men who have been crippled by our society and sending them 8,000 miles away to guarantee liberties in Southeast Asia which they have not found in southwest Georgia or in East Harlem." Two figures as different as King and Muhammad Ali refused to support the war, and such actions caused veterans to wonder if they had been wise to go to Vietnam in the first place.

Not only had African-Americans been ordered to participate in a war many considered immoral, but they also had seen or been a part of racial confrontations. Dissident African-American soldiers were given less-than-honorable discharges, and they discovered that this "bad paper" made for

Vietnam veteran Eugene Brice raises his flag while marching in the Vietnam Veterans' parade down Constitution Avenue in Washington, D.C., in 1982. Some vets have had problems readjusting to civilian society.

few jobs back home and that the military had taught them no skills. A number of African-Americans returned from Vietnam addicted to heroin, with alcohol problems, or with a dependence on marijuana.

Hispanic veterans also faced unemployment. Conditions were worse in the United States when they returned than when they had left.

Just as no two soldiers had the same experience in Vietnam, no two veterans had exact postwar experiences. Posttraumatic stress disorder affected a larger percentage of African- and Hispanic-Americans than whites. Native American veterans suffered problems with alcohol to a larger extent than Natives who did not serve. Many U.S. minority members sympathized with the Vietnamese to a greater extent than did European-Americans. Burning Vietnamese civilians out of their village "is what they did to my people one hundred years ago," said a Native American soldier who served in Vietnam.

Dealing with the Veterans Administration

Vets complained, and government research showed they had the right. Despite the propaganda, employers seldom sought out veterans when there were jobs. No "hire the vet" program was undertaken until 1971. Unemployment among veterans aged twenty to twenty-four averaged 13 percent, as against 11 percent for nonveterans, in 1970. Unemployment among African-American vets reached 20 percent, compared to 13 to 17 percent for Black nonvets. Wages likewise were tilted against those who served: $125 weekly on the average for African-American veterans versus $135 a week for nonvets. As many as two hundred thousand veterans of all races

Stories of the war

For one Vietnam veteran, whose father served in World War II, there is one big difference in their experiences. "My dad read books and watched movies to reinforce the good feeling he had about his World War II service," the vet said. "I read books and watch movies to try to find answers, to try to figure out what really happened over there." Fortunately, there are many sources for veterans and nonveterans alike. Outstanding nonfiction includes *Dispatches* by Michael Herr, which gives a sense of what "America's rock 'n' roll war" was really all about. A good overview is offered in *Vietnam: A History* by Stanley Karnow. This fact-filled work was a national bestseller and was written as a companion to the Public Broadcasting Service television series about the war.

That series is available on videotape in many libraries. It uses the same dramatic news footage that was delivered into American living rooms for more evenings than U.S. residents cared to think about. Movies dramatizing the war include *The Deer Hunter, Apocalypse Now, Platoon,* and *Full Metal Jacket.* Works of fiction range from the National Book Award-winning *Dog Soldiers*, a story about heroin, Vietnam, and the Vietnam era by Robert Stone, to *The Thirteenth Valley*, an action tale by Robert Del Vecchio. Tim O'Brien has written several highly praised works of fiction about Vietnam that use symbols to attempt explanations of what went on.

Two soldiers wounded in Persian Gulf War fighting visit the Vietnam Veterans' Memorial in Washington, D.C., in 1991.

crowded unemployment offices nationwide in the early seventies. They also crowded Veterans Administration (VA) facilities. The ranks of unemployed and disabled veterans knew no boundaries by race, class, or military status. White southern Protestants were there along with everyone else. These people had been considered the cream of the military, their "power elite."

Hawk or dove, the Vietnam veteran felt cheated. Consequently, Vietnam vets were the least inclined to take advantage of VA help with higher education. And for those who did, benefits failed to keep up with the climbing cost of education. Only one vet in four returned to any form of schooling.

Alhough Vietnam-era veterans were buffeted by rising costs, there were many VA programs designed for them. They included disability compensation, disability pension, education assistance, life insurance, home loans, vocational rehabilitation, hospitalization, and eventually, employment assistance. Those without money who were addicted to drugs often turned up at a VA hospital, feeling that treatment or possible access to prescribed medicines were better than the fate that awaited them on the streets. Psychological counseling, rather scarce in Vietnam, was generally available at VA centers.

A number of vets have helped themselves by helping each other. Under the guidance of one or more mental health professionals, groups of veterans meet on a regular basis to help rid each other of the demons that continue to haunt them. These meetings can be an important safety net. Most veterans determined to put Vietnam out of their minds have made an effort to get on with their lives without seeking outside help.

Others Leave the New Vietnam

The immediate postwar period was a difficult one for all Vietnamese as several disappointing harvests resulted in there being insufficient food to go around. The North Vietnamese treated their valiant Vietcong allies as their inferiors, filling all of the important government posts with northerners. Shopkeepers and merchants were ordered to share all they had, and businesses such as nightclubs, bars, restaurants, and newspapers in Ho Chi Minh City (formerly Saigon) were ordered closed. Malnutrition was common, and the mortality rate among children climbed.

Many people capable of doing so fled Vietnam. Those with money found reliable boats that would take them away. Those with little money boarded leaky, dangerous vessels for any destination, so long as it was away from Vietnam. Those without funds could hope that relatives who had departed earlier might send them money to leave. The government hazed persons who wanted to flee, forcing them to give up all or most of their belongings. Some Vietnamese were robbed on the high seas and

Nguyen Van Duc (center) and Tran Van Dung (right) are two of thirty-one Amerasian children in an orphanage in Ho Chi Minh City in 1982. Restrictive U.S. laws prevented many of the children from coming to the United States, and they were often shunned by the Vietnamese.

either killed or left to die of thirst or drowning. Refugee camps in Malaysia, Hong Kong, and Thailand were swollen with those who made it to a foreign shore — only to be held for months or even years.

Vietnamese and especially members of the Hmong minority from Laos managed to get to the United States in some numbers. The Vietnamese most often settled in California or along the shore of the Gulf of Mexico. They became restaurant owners, fishers, grocers, or took up other occupations. Hmong parents, who had lived simple, rural lives in Laos, had an especially hard time adjusting to the faster pace of life in the United States. Most children of these people seemed to do well in school and quickly learned how their adopted country worked. A few teenagers fell in with gangs in larger cities such as Los Angeles, where armed Cambodians or Vietnamese competed with African- or Hispanic-Americans for turf.

An ethnic Vietnamese family flees Phnom Penh, Cambodia, in 1993. An estimated one thousand boats carrying Vietnamese settlers moved down the Tonle Bassac River to meet a convoy headed for Vietnam. Tension between Cambodians and Vietnamese remains high.

Orphans and Boat People

An estimated fifteen thousand children of American and Vietnamese parents remained in Vietnam. Many had been orphaned. They were looked down upon by the Vietnamese, who called them "bui doi," or "dust of life." Their mothers often had been forced by circumstances into prostitution, and these young people were the result. They grazed for food and other needs among scrapheaps because not even their relatives wanted them around as reminders of the war. Since the end of the war, efforts have been largely successful in moving many of these orphans to new lives in the United States. More than 300,000 children were orphaned by the war, and there were 131,000 war widows.

Names on a Wall

There are 58,196 names inscribed on the the thick black granite of the Vietnam Veterans Memorial in Washington, D.C., even though the exact number probably is not correct or even known. Several years ago, one veteran listed as dead by the government found his own name inscribed on this memorial, which draws more visitors each year than any other of the capital's 150 national monuments. The memorial displays the names of the dead and the missing from more than a decade of war in Vietnam.

A Maryland Vietnam veteran, Jan Scruggs, got the concept for a monument in 1979. He conceived the idea of putting the name of every dead American soldier on a memorial, and he wanted it to be constructed without using government money. Land in Washington was set aside, and a nationwide competition was held for the best design. The contest was won by a female, Chinese-American, Harvard University student named Maya Linn, who designed a low, black, shiny, chevron-shaped wall. It stayed in the judges' minds more than any of the other fourteen hundred entries.

The wall had some opposition, from wealthy businessman Ross Perot to James Watt, then the secretary of the interior. But others garnered public support for the memorial, including retired General William Westmoreland and members of the American Legion, who alone raised one million dollars for the memorial. Some 275,000 people contributed money for building the monument.

Ground was broken in March 1982, and the wall and statue nearby were dedicated on November 13, 1982. Thousand of veterans, able and disabled, rich and poor, traveled to Washington to join a parade and witness the dedication and surrounding events. They were joined by parents who had lost sons, wives who had lost husbands, and children who had lost fathers. Names of the fallen were read aloud in a nearby church. Many veterans who had been unable to face the issue of Vietnam went home with their heads held higher.

The wall is eerie and somber, yet it continues to draw thousands each year. They leave notes to those whose names appear, along with many other poignant offerings. Two Medals of Honor have been left at the wall, along with teddy bears, boots, flowers and wreaths, love notes, phonograph records and tapes, and photos. The National Park Service collects the gifts and sometimes shows them in a traveling display.

A diamond-shaped mark is engraved beside the name of each soldier confirmed dead. The missing are marked with a cross. If remains of missing individuals are found, a diamond is inscribed over the cross. There are 2,214 soldiers still missing. If a missing soldier should return alive, a halo will be engraved above the cross. There are no halos on the wall to this day.

Is the War Over?

The issue of POWs and MIAs is one that did not go away. Were there Americans still being held against their will in Vietnam? The odds with each passing year grew increasingly slim — prisoners are the last to be fed or medicated, and Vietnam and Laos returned the American remains as they were found. By 1990, groups of U.S. veterans were routinely permitted to search for evidence of missing soldiers inside Vietnamese and Laotian borders. No living American prisoner has ever been found. With more and more Americans desirous of putting the war behind them, Vietnam in the 1990s was admitted to the U.S.-controlled World Bank. American investments followed immediately after a trade embargo was lifted.

Is the war over? Not for those who lost loved ones. Not for veterans who are wracked by pain or those who cannot forget the horror of their involvement. Not for Americans of Vietnamese or Laotian or Cambodia descent, who may be U.S. citizens but who are treated differently than their European-American counterparts. Not for widows and orphans on both sides, deprived of income, companionship, and love. And not for the United States as a whole, which remains divided between those who realize the country lost the war and those who believe the war could have been won. It is probably accurate to state that the Vietnam War will affect Americans until the last veteran of that terrible war is laid to rest.

Remains of American soldiers are saluted as they are moved toward U.S. aircraft outside Phnom Penh, Cambodia, in 1992. Relations between the United States and Southeast Asia nations continue to be influenced by the war and its aftermath.

A.D. 967   Emperor Dinh Bo Linh takes the throne of what would become Vietnam after one thousand years of domination by China

1428   The Chinese recognize Vietnam as an independent state

1600   French Roman Catholic missionaries arrive in Vietnam, teaching Christianity to the largely Buddhist population

1802   Emperor Gia Long unifies the country, which had split apart because of several large and small conflicts

1847   French and Vietnamese clash near modern-day Danang; Emperor Tu Duc vows to wipe out Christianity in Vietnam

1861   French forces take Saigon

1887   France creates the Indochinese Union, made up of Vietnam and Cambodia

1930   Ho Chi Minh and his comrades found the Indochinese Communist Party, based in Hong Kong

1940   Japan occupies Indochina but leaves the French administration in place

1944   Vo Nguyen Giap founds the Vietminh army, which will oppose the French presence in Indochina

1946   France returns to Vietnam

1954   The French are defeated by the Vietminh at Dien Bien Phu and prepare to give up their claim to Indochina

1955   The United States begins to send aid to South Vietnam and to train its troops

1963   President Ngo Dinh Diem is assassinated as South Vietnamese military personnel try to take control of the government; U.S. President John F. Kennedy is slain three weeks later

1964   U.S. aircraft attack North Vietnam following the apparent attack by North Vietnamese boats on a U.S. Navy ship, the *Maddox*

1965   U.S. troop strength in Vietnam at the end of this year reaches two hundred thousand

1966   U.S. troop strength stands at four hundred thousand by year's end

1967   Secretary of Defense Robert McNamara tells U.S. senators that the massive bombing of North Vietnam is ineffective

1968   Vietcong and North Vietnamese troops launch the Tet Offensive in January; prior to these attacks, most Americans had believed that the United States was winning the war; the number of troops at the end of the year is 540,000; Martin Luther King is slain; his death sparks riots in major U.S. cities

1969   New President Richard M. Nixon approves the secret bombing of Cambodia; antiwar demonstrations in the United States grow in size and frequency; details of a massacre of civilians by U.S. forces at My Lai are revealed

1970   National Guard troops kill four protesting students at Kent State University in Ohio; the slain students were demonstrating against the U.S. invasion of Cambodia

1971   U.S. troop strength sinks to 140,000 at the end of the year

1972	Nixon orders intense bombing of Hanoi and Haiphon, North Vietnam, to pressure the North Vietnamese to complete peace talks in Paris
1973	The last U.S. troops leave Vietnam on March 29, and the final known U.S. prisoner of war is released on April 1
1974	After several months of little or no action, the war flares again in January; Richard Nixon resigns the presidency to avoid impeachment proceedings following the scandal in his presidency known as Watergate; Gerald Ford is sworn in as president
1975	Saigon falls to communist forces on April 30 after months of military and civilian deaths in the south
1977	President Jimmy Carter pardons ten thousand U.S. men who evaded the draft
1982	The Vietnam Veterans Memorial is dedicated in Washington, D.C.

GLOSSARY

Agent Orange	a defoliant named after the orange barrels in which it was shipped; the substance was sprayed from aircraft and later was believed to have caused illness and even eventual death among U.S. and Vietnamese personnel in the vicinity
Central Intelligence Agency (CIA)	an agency, which is part of the U.S. government, whose mission is to gather information on the United States' friends and foes outside the country for officials to analyze and act upon in Washington, D.C.; the CIA operated in Southeast Asia since World War II; they conducted a secret war in Laos and helped sabotage North Vietnam's heavy industry
Cold War	confrontations between communist and noncommunist countries from 1946 through about 1990; these were wars of words, with the constant threat of nuclear weapons on both sides
communism	a form of government in which all goods are held in common; all land and other means of production and distribution are held by the government, which is defined as all citizens; following the dissolution of the Soviet Union and the departure of communist governments in Poland, Rumania, and most other Eastern European nations, by the mid-1990s China, Cuba, North Korea, and Vietnam were left as virtually the only remaining states practicing communism
conscientious objector	a person who, for religious reasons, will not carry a weapon as part of a military unit; conscientious objectors served as medics and in other noncombat jobs during the Vietnam War
deferment	as used during the Vietnam War era, a permit that allowed students to stay in school rather than be drafted out of the classroom; deferment decisions were made by local Selective Service (draft board) offices
defoliants	chemicals used to kill vegetation; use of the chemicals was intended to deny the North Vietnamese Army (NVA) and the Vietcong (VC) places to hide
demilitarized zone (DMZ)	the line, draw in Geneva, Switzerland, in 1954, that divided North and South Vietnam; during the war, the DMZ became one of the most dangerous, bomb-rocked sites in Vietnam
dove	any American who was against U.S. military involvement in Vietnam
escalation	as used during the Vietnam War, the planned, step-by-step increase in activity by the U.S. government; escalation took the form of sending more and more weapons and troops to Vietnam

frag	to injure or kill another soldier, usually an officer, with a fragmentation grenade; grenades can be thrown or used as booby traps, sometimes activated by a trip wire
GI	a U.S. soldier; the abbreviation stands for Government Issue and has been used for decades to note any American in military uniform
guerrillas	civilians who band together to fight, usually against their own government or a foreign force; the Vietcong, which fought against the South Vietnamese government and its U.S. allies, was such an organization, since VC were South Vietnamese civilians
hawk	any American who favored U.S. military involvement in Vietnam
Ho Chi Minh Trail	a path hundreds of miles long that led from North Vietnam, through Laos and Cambodia, into western South Vietnam; used by NVA soldiers to infiltrate the south
infiltration	during the era of the Vietnam War, the entry into South Vietnam by North Vietnamese Army troops, usually traveling down the Ho Chi Minh Trail
M-16	the standard U.S. Army automatic rifle during the Vietnam War; the weapon weighed only six pounds, carried a twenty-round clip of ammunition, and worked well if kept clean
mortar	a short-barreled cannon that fires a shell at high angles; mortars were used in Vietnam because two or three men could carry them and they could be quickly fired and moved
napalm	jellied fuel packed in bombs that explode on impact; the explosion creates a sticky, flowing fire that can cause severe or fatal burns; napalm was introduced in Vietnam by French forces and used by the United States
shrapnel	hot, flying, jagged pieces of metal thrown by an exploding shell, bomb, or grenade
Tet	the Vietnamese new year; the date for this yearly celebration depends on the full moon but is usually late January or early February; the Tet Offensive was the 1968 attack by North Vietnamese Army and Vietcong forces, timed to coincide with Tet celebrations across the south
Vietcong	guerrilla forces fighting against South Vietnamese government troops and against U.S. advisors and troops; the military arm of the National Front for the Liberation of Vietnam, the umbrella political group of South Vietnamese opposed to the government of South Vietnam
Vietminh	forces organized by Ho Chi Minh to fight the Japanese and then the French; the Vietminh later became the North Vietnamese Army

FURTHER READING

Garland, Sherry. *Rebuilding a Nation* (*Discovering Our Heritage* series). Minneapolis: Dillon Press, 1990.

Fincher, E. B. *The Vietnam War*. New York: Franklin Watts, 1980.

Huynh Quang Nhuong. *The Land I Lost*. New York: Harper and Row, Publishers, 1986.

Jacobsen, Karen. *Vietnam (A New True Book)*. Chicago: Children's Press, 1992.

Page, Tim. *Ten Years After: Vietnam Today*. New York: Alfred Knopf, 1987.

Vietnam in Pictures (*Visual Geography* series). Minneapolis: Lerner Publications Company, 1994.

Wright, David. *Vietnam (Enchantment of the World* series). Chicago: Children's Press, 1989.

Wright, David. *War in Vietnam*, Vols. I-IV. Chicago: Children's Press, 1989.

Wright, David. *The Story of the Vietnam Memorial*, Children's Press, Chicago, 1989.

Zinn, Howard. *A People's History of the United States*. New York: Harper and Row, Publishers, 1980.

80